PRESTO

Pressure Cooker Recipes

Publications International, Ltd.

Louis Weber, CEO
Publications International, Ltd.
7373 North Cicero Avenue
Lincolnwood, IL 60712

Permission is never granted for commercial purposes.

Presto® and the Presto® logo are registered trademarks of National Presto Industries, Inc.

Front cover photography and photography on pages 11, 15, 29, 31, 33, 35, 37, 55, 63, 79, 81, 95, 97, 115, 117, 121, 129, 131, 133, and 137 shot at PIL Photo Studio.

Photographers: Justin Paris, Annemarie Zelasko
Photographers' Assistant: Lauren Kessler
Prop Stylist: Paula Walters
Food Stylists: Walter Moeller, Josephine Orba, Mary-Helen Steindler
Assistant Food Stylists: Sheila Grannen, Breana Moeller

Pictured on the front cover: Bacon and Stout Short Ribs *(page 28).*

Pictured on the back cover: Four-Bean Chili Stew *(page 98),* Honey Ginger Ribs *(page 54),* and Mocha Custard *(page 128).*

Some of the products listed in this publication may be in limited distribution.

ISBN-13: 978-1-4508-2407-1
ISBN-10: 1-4508-2407-2

Library of Congress Control Number: 2011922366

Manufactured in China.

8 7 6 5 4 3 2 1

Table of Contents

Cooking Under Pressure, *the Easy Way*

How would you like to use a cooking method that saves time and money, while making the most of the nutrition and flavor of your food? If that sounds appealing, then you're going to enjoy using a Presto® pressure cooker.

If you're familiar with pressure cookers, you know they cook foods more quickly than regular stovetop cooking and yield tender results, even from the toughest cuts of meat. The faster cooking time saves energy and retains vitamins that can be lost when foods are cooked longer.

And if you're new to pressure cooking, you'll be pleasantly surprised at the variety of dishes you can prepare quickly and easily. Once you try the recipes in this cookbook, you'll wonder how you ever got along without a pressure cooker.

Pressure Cooking 101

Basically, a pressure cooker is a pot that uses a locking cover with a rubber sealing ring. By allowing steam to escape only through the vent pipe in the cover, the pressure cooker allows steam to build inside the pot to temperatures that are higher than the boiling point of 212°F. At 15 pounds per square inch (psi), the temperature inside a pressure cooker is about 250°F. This higher temperature cooks food faster, while the steam produces moist, tender foods.

To control the amount of pressure inside the pot, a pressure regulator (also called a "jiggler") sits on the vent pipe. By covering the hole in the vent pipe, the pressure regulator allows the pressure to reach a standard of 15 psi for consistent cooking times and recipe results. Once the pressure reaches 15 psi, the pressure regulator begins to rock, allowing excess pressure to be released to maintain a steady 15 psi.

To prevent the cooker from being opened until the built-up pressure inside is safely released, a cover lock in the handle rises to prevent the cover from being turned. The overpressure plug, a rubber plug on the cover, also pops up as the pressure rises.

A pressure cooker works on any kind of range (only stainless steel pressure cookers work on induction ranges). However, burners on some electric ranges may not cool down as quickly as necessary, so have a second burner ready at a lower heat setting. Continuing to cook at a heat setting that's too high will allow too much steam to escape, and may result in dishes that are dry or scorched.

PRESSURE REGULATOR

The removable weighted pressure regulator controls and maintains pressure inside the cooker. When it starts to rock, the standard cooking pressure of 15 psi has been reached.

VENT PIPE

The opening in the cover on which the pressure regulator is placed. It allows excess pressure to be released at a controlled rate. Always make sure the vent pipe is clear and not clogged before you start cooking.

SEALING RING

The rubber gasket placed in the cover forms a pressure-tight seal that allows pressure to build in the cooker. Store your pressure cooker with the cover inverted, or the sealing ring may become compressed and fail to seal properly.

AIR VENT/COVER LOCK

The opening in the handle that includes the lock pin. When pressure begins to build in the cooker, the lock pin rises to seal the cooker and to prevent it from being opened until the pressure inside has returned to normal.

OVERPRESSURE PLUG

A rubber plug on the lid, which also rises as the pressure inside the cooker builds. It acts as a safety device that will release the pressure if, for some reason, the vent pipe is clogged and can't release the pressure normally.

COVER HANDLE

The handle aligns so the cover lock can rise and drop, showing whether there is pressure in the cooker.

COOKING RACK

The removable rack holds foods out of the cooking liquid for distinct flavors, but its use is optional if you prefer the food flavors to blend. It also should be used to position a cooking vessel, such as a bowl or pan, inside the cooker so it doesn't sit directly on the bottom.

Using the Pressure Cooker

The recipes in this cookbook provide step-by-step directions, so you can easily prepare tasty dishes in your Presto® pressure cooker—even if it's your first try. Here's a quick overview of the steps:

1 The recipe will provide a specific cooking method and time. Be sure to **add the required amount of liquid,** and use the cooking rack when indicated.

2 Make sure the vent pipe is not clogged; hold the cover up to the light and look through the vent pipe. If necessary, use a small brush or pipe cleaner to clean it.

3 Insert the sealing ring into the cover. Place the cover on the pressure cooker, aligning the mark on the handle with the mark on the cover. Applying downward pressure, turn the cover clockwise until the handles align and the cover lock clicks into place.

4 Place the pressure regulator on the vent pipe. For consistent results, **always start cooking on high heat.**

5 The cooking time begins when the pressure regulator begins to rock, indicating 15 psi has been reached. **Lower the heat** and continue cooking **with the pressure regulator rocking slowly.** To see and hear an example of the correct rocking motion that maintains consistent 15-psi pressure, visit http://discoverpressurecooking.com/tips.html.

6 Cook the food under pressure for the amount of time specified in the recipe; **use a timer for best results.** Then, cool the pressure cooker according to the method specified in the recipe.

Cooling the Pressure Cooker

If the recipe says **"cool cooker at once under cold running water,"** place the pressure cooker under a running faucet. Continue cooling under running water until the cover lock in the handle drops, indicating that the pressure has been released and the cover can be opened. If the recipe says **"remove from heat and let stand until cover lock drops,"** move the pressure cooker to an unheated burner and allow it to cool naturally. This may take 10 to 15 minutes, depending on how much food is in the cooker and how warm or cool it is in your kitchen.

When the cover lock has dropped, the pressure inside the cooker has returned to normal. **Don't remove the pressure regulator until the cover lock drops and pressure has returned to normal.** Remove the pressure regulator, open the cover, and follow any additional recipe directions.

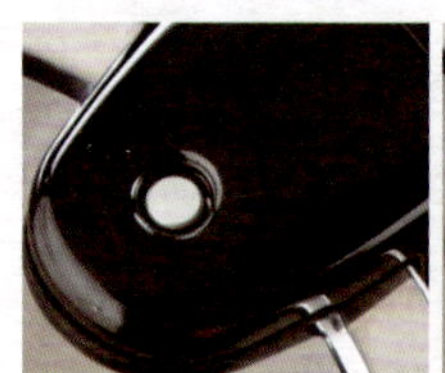

COVER LOCK UNDER PRESSURE

COVER LOCK DROPPED, PRESSURE RELEASED

Hints and Tips

✗ You can cook large or small quantities, but there must be space for steam to build, so don't fill the cooker more than $^2/_3$ full. Some foods, such as dry beans and peas, should not exceed the $^1/_2$-full mark on the inside of the cooker.

✗ Liquid is needed to generate steam to build pressure. However, some liquid will escape during the pressure cooking period. Recipes call for $^1/_2$ to 1 cup more liquid than needed for the finished dish. Although recipes use water, broth, wine, or beer, you also can try fruit or vegetable juices or other liquids.

✗ If a dish has more liquid than you prefer, continue simmering, uncovered, until it reaches the desired thickness. Or you may prefer to add flour or cornstarch, and cook and stir the liquid until it's thickened. You also can reduce the liquid a bit the next time you prepare the recipe. Be careful not to reduce it too much, though, or you may wind up with a scorched dish.

✗ Some recipes have a "0" cooking time. This means you should cool the cooker as soon as the pressure regulator begins to rock.

✗ To use steel or oven-safe glass pans or bowls in your Presto® pressure cooker, look for items no more than $7^1/_2$ inches in diameter and no higher than the $^2/_3$ mark when placed on the cooking rack. Most recipes in this cookbook were tested in metal bowls; for glass or ceramic bowls, increase the pressure cooking time 1 to 5 minutes, depending on the size of the vessel.

Foil Handle

To easily lower and raise a pan or bowl in the pressure cooker, use 12- to 18-inch-wide heavy-duty aluminum foil to make a lifting "handle." Tear off a piece of foil 30 inches long. Fold the piece lengthwise three times to make a long strip about 4 to 6 inches wide. Lay the strip on the countertop. Put the bowl in the center of the strip. Pull the ends up around the side of the bowl to lift it in and out of the cooker. Take care not to pinch the handle ends in the cooker lid (fold down the ends before putting the cover on the cooker).

About the recipes

Each recipe in this cookbook was tested in a 6-quart Presto® pressure cooker to determine the proper cooking time under pressure, as well as the best cooling method to yield tender and tasty results. However, because every range is a little different, keep track of the cooking time at 15 psi the first time you prepare a recipe. If the food isn't completely done to your taste after the recommended cooking time, close the cover, bring the cooker back up to pressure, and cook the dish 1 or 2 minutes longer. Then, make a note for the next time you prepare the dish.

Soups *and* Stocks

Potato Soup with Green Chiles & Cheese

makes 4 to 6 servings

1	tablespoon vegetable oil
1	medium onion, chopped
1	clove garlic, minced
1	tablespoon all-purpose flour
2	cups chopped unpeeled potatoes
2	cups chicken broth
$^1/_2$	teaspoon celery salt, divided
2	cups milk
1	can (4 ounces) diced green chiles, drained
$^3/_4$	cup (3 ounces) shredded Monterey Jack cheese
$^3/_4$	cup (3 ounces) shredded Colby or Cheddar cheese
	Salt and white pepper, to taste

1 Heat oil in cooker over medium heat. Cook and stir onion and garlic 4 minutes or until soft. Stir in flour. Stir in potatoes, broth, and $^1/_4$ teaspoon celery salt.

2 Close cover securely. Place pressure regulator on vent pipe. Continue cooking over **high** heat until pressure regulator begins to rock. **Lower heat and cook 5 minutes with pressure regulator rocking slowly.**

3 **Remove from heat and let stand until cover lock drops.** Open cooker. Stir in milk, chiles, and remaining $^1/_4$ teaspoon celery salt. Simmer, uncovered, 5 minutes. Add Monterey Jack and Colby cheeses; stir over low heat until cheeses melt. (Do not boil.) Season with salt and pepper.

Bean and Pasta Soup

makes 6 servings

1¼	cups dried navy beans
7	cups cold water, divided
3	slices bacon, finely chopped
1	onion, chopped
1	stalk celery, chopped
¾	pound smoked pork rib or neck bones, rinsed well under cold water
2	medium cloves garlic, minced
½	teaspoon dried thyme, crushed
½	teaspoon dried marjoram, crushed
¼	teaspoon black pepper
¾	cup uncooked small pasta shells
2	tablespoons chopped fresh parsley
	Salt, to taste
½	to 1 cup beef broth (optional)
	Grated Parmesan cheese (optional)

1 Rinse beans thoroughly in colander under cold running water, picking out any debris or blemished beans. Combine beans and 4 cups water. Soak 4 to 8 hours or overnight. After soaking, rinse and drain beans, and remove any loose skins.

2 Fry bacon in cooker over medium-high heat 2 minutes. Add onion and celery; cook and stir 3 minutes or until golden brown. Place bones, remaining 3 cups water, beans, garlic, thyme, marjoram, and pepper in cooker; stir to mix well.

3 Close cover securely. Place pressure regulator on vent pipe. Continue cooking over **high** heat until pressure regulator begins to rock. **Lower heat and cook 8 minutes with pressure regulator rocking slowly.**

4 **Remove from heat and let stand until cover lock drops.** Open cooker. Remove bones; set aside. Remove half of bean mixture with slotted spoon; place in blender or food processor. Add 2 tablespoons cooking liquid; process until smooth. Stir puréed bean mixture into soup. Bring soup to a boil over high heat. Stir in pasta. Reduce heat to medium-low. Simmer, uncovered, 10 minutes or until pasta is tender, stirring occasionally.

5 Remove meat from bones; chop and stir into soup. Discard bones. Stir in parsley and salt. If necessary, thin soup with broth. Serve with cheese, if desired.

New England Fish Chowder

¼	pound bacon, diced
1	cup chopped onion
½	cup chopped celery
2	cups water
2	cups diced russet potatoes
1	teaspoon dried dill
½	teaspoon dried thyme
½	teaspoon salt
½	teaspoon black pepper
1	bay leaf
1	pound cod, haddock, or halibut fillets, skinned, boned, and cut into 1-inch pieces*
2	tablespoons all-purpose flour
2	tablespoons water
2	cups milk or half-and-half

If fillets are very thin, cut into large pieces to prevent overcooking.

1 Fry bacon in cooker over medium heat until crisp. Remove bacon with slotted spoon to paper towels. Pour off all but 1 tablespoon fat.

2 Add onion and celery to cooker; cook and stir 3 minutes or until onion is soft. Add water, potatoes, dill, thyme, salt, pepper, and bay leaf; stir to mix well.

3 Close cover securely. Place pressure regulator on vent pipe. Continue cooking over **high** heat until pressure regulator begins to rock. **Lower heat and cook 5 minutes with pressure regulator rocking slowly.**

4 **Remove from heat and let stand until cover lock drops.** Open cooker. Stir in fish. Close cover securely. Place pressure regulator on vent pipe. Continue cooking over **high** heat until pressure regulator begins to rock. **Lower heat and cook 1 minute with pressure regulator rocking slowly.**

5 **Remove from heat and let stand until cover lock drops.** Open cooker. Stir in reserved bacon. Combine flour and water; stir into soup. Cook and stir, uncovered, over medium heat until thickened. Stir in milk; simmer over low heat 2 to 3 minutes or until warmed through. (Do not boil.) Remove bay leaf before serving.

Hearty White Bean Soup

1½	cups dried navy beans
8½	cups water, divided
2	cups chicken broth
1	cup chopped onions
1	cup chopped carrots
1	cup chopped red or green bell pepper
½	cup chopped celery
2	cloves garlic, minced
1	tablespoon olive oil
1	tablespoon chopped fresh marjoram or 1 teaspoon dried marjoram, crushed
1½	teaspoons chopped fresh thyme or ¾ teaspoon dried thyme, crushed
1	teaspoon salt
½	teaspoon ground cumin
¼	teaspoon black pepper
	French bread or 1½ cups croutons (optional)

1 Rinse beans thoroughly in colander under cold running water, picking out any debris or blemished beans. Combine beans and 4½ cups water. Soak 4 to 8 hours or overnight. After soaking, rinse and drain beans, and remove any loose skins.

2 Combine beans, remaining 4 cups water, broth, onions, carrots, bell pepper, celery, garlic, oil, marjoram, thyme, salt, cumin, and black pepper in cooker; stir to mix well.

3 Close cover securely. Place pressure regulator on vent pipe. Cook over **high** heat until pressure regulator begins to rock. **Lower heat and cook 3 minutes with pressure regulator rocking slowly.**

4 **Remove from heat and let stand until cover lock drops.** Open cooker. Serve soup with French bread, if desired.

Hearty Vegetable Soup

1	cup dried Great Northern beans
3	cups water
1	tablespoon olive oil
1	cup chopped onion
3/4	cup chopped carrots
3	cloves garlic, minced
4	cups coarsely chopped green cabbage
4	cups coarsely chopped unpeeled red potatoes
1	teaspoon dried rosemary
1/2	teaspoon black pepper
1/4	teaspoon salt
4	cups vegetable broth
1	can (14 1/2 ounces) diced tomatoes, undrained
	Grated Parmesan cheese (optional)

1 Rinse beans thoroughly in colander under cold running water, picking out any debris or blemished beans. Combine beans and water. Soak 4 to 8 hours or overnight. After soaking, rinse and drain beans, and remove any loose skins.

2 Heat oil in cooker over medium-high heat. Add onion and carrots; cook and stir 3 minutes or until soft. Add garlic; cook and stir 1 minute. Add cabbage, potatoes, rosemary, pepper, and salt; cook and stir 1 minute. Add beans, broth, and tomatoes; stir to mix well.

3 Close cover securely. Place pressure regulator on vent pipe. Continue cooking over **high** heat until pressure regulator begins to rock. **Lower heat and cook 3 minutes with pressure regulator rocking slowly.**

4 **Remove from heat and let stand until cover lock drops.** Open cooker. Serve with Parmesan cheese, if desired.

Oxtail Soup with Beer

2¹⁄₂	pounds meaty oxtails (beef or veal)
1	large onion, sliced
4	carrots, cut into 1-inch pieces, divided
3	stalks celery, cut into 1-inch pieces, divided
2	sprigs fresh parsley
5	whole black peppercorns
1	bay leaf
2	cups beef broth
1	cup dark beer
1	large russet potato, cut into 1-inch pieces
¹⁄₄	teaspoon salt
2	tablespoons chopped fresh parsley (optional)

1 Combine oxtails, onion, half of carrots, one-third of celery, parsley sprigs, peppercorns, and bay leaf in cooker. Pour broth and beer over mixture.

2 Close cover securely. Place pressure regulator on vent pipe. Cook over **high** heat until pressure regulator begins to rock. **Lower heat and cook 20 minutes with pressure regulator rocking slowly.**

3 **Cool cooker at once under cold running water.** Open cooker. Remove oxtails; set aside to cool. Strain broth through large sieve or colander; press vegetables lightly with slotted spoon to extract all liquid. Discard vegetables. Remove meat from oxtails when cool enough to handle, discarding fat and bones.

4 Wipe cooker with paper towels, if necessary. Return broth to cooker. Add remaining half of carrots, two-thirds of celery, and potato. Cook over **high** heat until pressure regulator begins to rock. **Lower heat and cook 3 minutes with pressure regulator rocking slowly.**

5 **Cool cooker at once under cold running water.** Open cooker. Add meat to soup. Stir in salt. Simmer, uncovered, until meat is heated through. Garnish with chopped parsley, if desired.

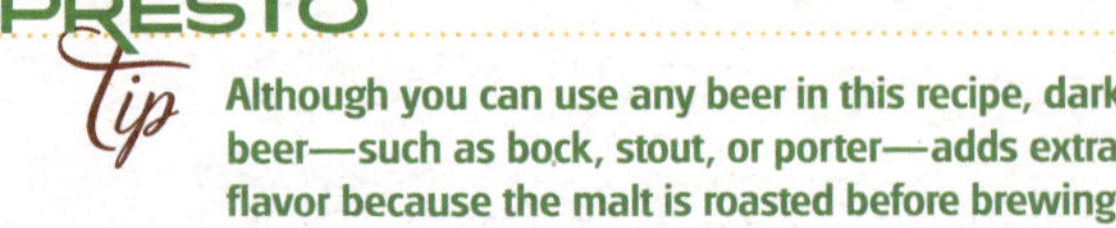

PRESTO Tip Although you can use any beer in this recipe, dark beer—such as bock, stout, or porter—adds extra flavor because the malt is roasted before brewing.

Spicy Squash and Chicken Soup

makes 4 servings

1	tablespoon vegetable oil
1	small onion, finely chopped
1	stalk celery, finely chopped
2	cups delicata or butternut squash (about 1 small), cut into 1-inch cubes
2	cups chicken broth
1	can (about 14 ounces) diced tomatoes with chiles
1	cup chopped cooked chicken
$\frac{1}{2}$	teaspoon ground ginger
$\frac{1}{4}$	teaspoon salt
$\frac{1}{8}$	teaspoon ground cumin
$\frac{1}{8}$	teaspoon black pepper
2	teaspoons lime juice
	Fresh parsley or cilantro sprigs (optional)

1 Heat oil in cooker over medium heat. Cook and stir onion and celery 5 minutes or until soft. Stir in squash, broth, tomatoes, chicken, ginger, salt, cumin, and pepper.

2 Close cover securely. Place pressure regulator on vent pipe. Continue cooking over **high** heat until pressure regulator begins to rock. **Lower heat and cook 10 minutes with pressure regulator rocking slowly.**

3 **Cool cooker at once under cold running water.** Open cooker. Stir in lime juice. Garnish with parsley, if desired.

PRESTO
Tip

Delicata and butternut are two types of winter squash. Delicata is an elongated creamy-yellow squash with green striations. Butternut is a long light-orange squash. Both have hard skins. To use, cut the squash lengthwise, scoop out the seeds, peel, and cut into cubes.

Creamy Carrot Soup

makes 4 servings

2	teaspoons butter
1/3	cup chopped onion
1	tablespoon chopped fresh ginger
1	pound baby carrots, or carrots cut into 2-inch pieces
1/2	teaspoon salt
1/4	teaspoon black pepper
3	cups vegetable broth
1/4	cup whipping cream
1/4	cup orange juice
	Pinch ground nutmeg
4	tablespoons sour cream

1 Melt butter in cooker over medium-high heat. Add onion and ginger; cook and stir 1 minute or until ginger is fragrant. Add carrots, salt, and pepper; cook and stir 2 minutes. Stir in broth.

2 Close cover securely. Place pressure regulator on vent pipe. Continue cooking over **high** heat until pressure regulator begins to rock. **Lower heat and cook 10 minutes with pressure regulator rocking slowly.**

3 **Remove from heat and let stand until cover lock drops.** Open cooker. Purée soup in cooker with immersion blender until smooth, or carefully process in 2-cup batches in blender. Return soup to cooker. Stir in whipping cream, orange juice, and nutmeg. Simmer over low heat until heated through. (Do not boil.) If necessary, thin soup with additional broth. Top soup with sour cream just before serving.

Rich Beef Stock

2	pounds meaty beef bones, rinsed well under cold water
$2^{1}/_{2}$	tablespoons ($1^{1}/_{2}$ ounces) tomato paste
1	large onion, top and roots removed, brown outer skin intact, cut into wedges
1	large carrot, cut in half
2	stalks celery, cut in half
$4^{1}/_{4}$	cups cold water, divided
4	sprigs fresh parsley
1	bay leaf
$^{1}/_{2}$	teaspoon dried thyme, crushed
3	whole black peppercorns
1	whole clove
$^{1}/_{8}$	teaspoon salt

1 Preheat oven to 450°F. Arrange bones in small roasting pan. Brown bones in oven 30 minutes, turning once.

2 Remove roasting pan from oven. Spread tomato paste over bones. Arrange onion, carrot, and celery over bones. Return pan to oven; roast bones and vegetables 30 minutes longer.

3 Transfer bones and vegetables to cooker. Skim excess fat from roasting pan and discard. Pour 1 cup water into pan. Cook and stir over medium-high heat, scraping up browned bits from bottom of pan, 2 to 3 minutes or until mixture has reduced to about $^{1}/_{2}$ cup liquid. Transfer to cooker. Add remaining $3^{1}/_{4}$ cups water, parsley, bay leaf, thyme, peppercorns, clove, and salt; stir to mix well.

4 Close cover securely. Place pressure regulator on vent pipe. Cook over **high** heat until pressure regulator begins to rock. **Lower heat and cook 60 minutes with pressure regulator rocking slowly.**

5 **Remove from heat and let stand until cover lock drops.** Open cooker. Remove large bones; set aside. Strain stock through large sieve or colander lined with several layers of damp cheesecloth; press vegetables lightly with slotted spoon to extract all liquid. Remove any meat from bones; reserve for another use. Discard bones and vegetables. Use stock immediately, or refrigerate in tightly covered container up to three days. Skim and discard fat before using in recipes calling for beef stock or broth.

Chicken Stock

4	cups water
1	small onion, cut into quarters
1	clove garlic, cut in half
1	bay leaf
3	sprigs fresh parsley
$1/2$	teaspoon salt
$1/4$	teaspoon ground cumin
3	whole black peppercorns
1	chicken (3 to 4 pounds), cut in half

1 Pour water into cooker. Stir in onion, garlic, bay leaf, parsley, salt, cumin, and peppercorns. Place chicken in cooker.

2 Close cover securely. Place pressure regulator on vent pipe. Cook over **high** heat until pressure regulator begins to rock. **Lower heat and cook 15 minutes with pressure regulator rocking slowly.**

3 **Remove from heat and let stand until cover lock drops.** Open cooker. Remove chicken with slotted spoon; let cool. Strain stock through large sieve or colander lined with several layers of damp cheesecloth. Discard solids. Use stock immediately, or refrigerate in tightly covered container up to three days. Skim and discard fat before using in recipes calling for chicken stock or broth.

4 Remove chicken meat from bones; discard skin and bones. Use in recipes calling for cooked chicken.

PRESTO
Tip

Use the cooked chicken to make the Spicy Squash and Chicken Soup on page 20. Or, make Chicken Noodle Soup: add 1 cup uncooked noodles, $3/4$ cup sliced carrots, $1/2$ cup chopped onion, and $1/4$ cup chopped celery to the stock; simmer, uncovered, 10 to 15 minutes or until the noodles and vegetables are cooked. Stir in 1 cup cooked chicken, and simmer until warmed through.

Vegetable Stock

2	leeks
2	tablespoons vegetable oil
2	medium onions, tops and roots removed, brown outer skin intact, cut into wedges
3	stalks celery, cut into 2-inch pieces
8	cups cold water
6	medium carrots, cut into 1-inch pieces
1	turnip, peeled, cut into chunks (optional)
2	cloves garlic, crushed
4	sprigs fresh parsley
1	teaspoon dried thyme, crushed
$1/8$	teaspoon salt
$1/8$	teaspoon black pepper
2	bay leaves

PRESTO Tip Stock also may be frozen in airtight freezer containers for two to three months.

1 Remove any withered outer leaves from leeks. Cut off leaf tops down to where dark green begins to pale; discard tops. Cut off roots; make deep cut into each leek to within an inch of root end. Separate layers slightly and wash thoroughly under cold running water to remove any embedded soil.

2 Heat oil in cooker over medium heat. Cook and stir leeks, onions, and celery 5 minutes or until soft. Add water, carrots, turnip (if desired), garlic, parsley, thyme, salt, pepper, and bay leaves.

3 Close cover securely. Place pressure regulator on vent pipe. Continue cooking over **high** heat until pressure regulator begins to rock. **Lower heat and cook 30 minutes with pressure regulator rocking slowly.**

4 **Remove from heat and let stand until cover lock drops.** Open cooker. Strain stock through large sieve or colander; press vegetables lightly with slotted spoon to extract all liquid. Discard vegetables. Use stock immediately, or refrigerate in airtight container up to two days.

A Bounty of Beef

Onion-Wine Pot Roast

makes 6 servings

1	boneless beef chuck roast (about 3 pounds), well trimmed
2	pounds yellow onions, cut in half and thinly sliced
2	cups red wine, such as cabernet sauvignon or merlot
1	teaspoon salt
$\frac{1}{2}$	teaspoon black pepper

1 Place beef, onions, wine, salt, and pepper in cooker. Close cover securely. Place pressure regulator on vent pipe. Cook over **high** heat until pressure regulator begins to rock. **Lower heat and cook 45 minutes with pressure regulator rocking slowly.**

2 **Remove from heat and let stand until cover lock drops.** Open cooker. Skim fat from juices and serve with beef. If necessary, simmer sauce, uncovered, to desired thickness.

PRESTO
Tip

This flavorful pot roast is easy to make. But if you prefer the flavor added by browning, season the beef with the salt and pepper first, then heat 1 tablespoon olive oil to brown it on both sides. Remove the beef, add 1 more tablespoon of olive oil, and cook the onions until they're golden. Add the wine and scrape up the browned bits before returning the beef and any juices to the cooker. Proceed as directed.

Bacon and Stout Short Ribs

4	pounds bone-in beef short ribs, well trimmed, and cut into 3-inch pieces
1/2	teaspoon black pepper
6	slices (about 6 ounces) thick-cut bacon, chopped
1	large onion, sliced
1	tablespoon tomato paste
1	bottle (12 ounces) stout, dark beer, or ale
1	cup beef or chicken broth
2	tablespoons spicy brown mustard
1	bay leaf
3	tablespoons cold water
2	tablespoons all-purpose flour
2	tablespoons finely chopped parsley
	Hot mashed potatoes or cooked egg noodles (optional)

1 Season ribs with pepper; set aside. Fry bacon in cooker over medium heat until crisp. Remove bacon with slotted spoon to paper towels. Brown short ribs a few at a time in bacon drippings; transfer to plate.

2 Pour off all but 1 tablespoon fat. Cook and stir onion 3 minutes or until golden brown. Stir in tomato paste until smooth. Stir in stout, broth, mustard, reserved bacon, and bay leaf. Return short ribs to cooker.

3 Close cover securely. Place pressure regulator on vent pipe. Continue cooking over **high** heat until pressure regulator begins to rock. **Lower heat and cook 30 minutes with pressure regulator rocking slowly.**

4 **Remove from heat and let stand until cover lock drops.** Open cooker. Remove short ribs from cooker; keep warm. Combine water and flour; add to sauce. Cook and stir sauce, uncovered, to desired thickness. Stir in parsley. Remove bay leaf before serving sauce with short ribs and mashed potatoes, if desired.

PRESTO
Tip

If you use instant-blending flour for thickening, you normally don't need to mix it with water before adding it to the sauce. For best results, follow the directions on the package.

Tasty Traditional Goulash

½	cup all-purpose flour
2	teaspoons salt
1	teaspoon black pepper
2	pounds boneless beef chuck shoulder, cut into bite-size pieces
3	to 4 tablespoons vegetable oil, divided
2	shallots or 1 medium onion, finely chopped
3	cloves garlic, finely chopped
1	can (about 28 ounces) diced tomatoes, undrained
1	tablespoon ground paprika
1	cup water
1	tablespoon fresh chopped parsley or 1 teaspoon dried parsley flakes
1	teaspoon dried thyme
2	bay leaves
½	cup sour cream, or to taste
	Hot cooked egg noodles
	Chopped fresh dill (optional)

1 Combine flour, salt, and pepper in large resealable plastic food storage bag. Add beef and toss to coat evenly; shake off excess flour mixture.

2 Heat 1 tablespoon oil in cooker over medium-high heat. Brown one-third of beef evenly on all sides. Transfer beef from cooker to plate; repeat with remaining oil and beef.

3 Add remaining 1 tablespoon oil to cooker, if necessary. Cook and stir shallots and garlic over medium heat 2 minutes or until soft. Add tomatoes and paprika; cook and stir 2 minutes, scraping up browned bits from bottom of cooker. Place beef and any juices in cooker. Stir in water, parsley, thyme, and bay leaves.

4 Close cover securely. Place pressure regulator on vent pipe. Continue cooking over **high** heat until pressure regulator begins to rock. **Lower heat and cook 15 minutes with pressure regulator rocking slowly.**

5 **Remove from heat and let stand until cover lock drops.** Open cooker and adjust salt and pepper, to taste. Stir in sour cream; cook and stir over low heat 5 minutes or until warmed through. (Do not boil.) Remove bay leaf before serving over noodles. Garnish with dill, if desired.

Espresso-Laced Pot Roast

makes 6 to 8 servings

1	tablespoon espresso powder
1	tablespoon firmly packed brown sugar
¹/₂	teaspoon salt
¹/₂	teaspoon black pepper
1	boneless beef chuck pot roast (2 to 2¹/₂ pounds)
1¹/₂	tablespoons vegetable oil or bacon drippings
1	can (14¹/₂ ounces) beef broth
1	large onion, coarsely chopped
¹/₂	teaspoon dried thyme
2	bay leaves
1	pound carrots, cut into 1-inch chunks
6	to 8 red potatoes, cut into quarters
3	tablespoons cold water
2	tablespoons all-purpose flour

1 Combine espresso, brown sugar, salt, and pepper in small bowl. Rub mixture into all surfaces of beef.

2 Heat oil in cooker over medium heat. Brown beef on both sides, about 4 minutes. Add broth, onion, thyme, and bay leaves.

3 Close cover securely. Place pressure regulator on vent pipe. Continue cooking over **high** heat until pressure regulator begins to rock. **Lower heat and cook 35 minutes with pressure regulator rocking slowly.**

4 **Cool cooker at once under cold running water.** Open cooker. Add carrots and potatoes. Close cover securely. Place pressure regulator on vent pipe. Continue cooking over **high** heat until pressure regulator begins to rock. **Lower heat and cook 3 minutes with pressure regulator rocking slowly.**

5 **Cool cooker at once under cold running water.** Open cooker. Remove vegetables and beef; keep warm. Combine water and flour; add to sauce. Cook and stir sauce, uncovered, to desired thickness. Remove bay leaves before serving sauce over beef and vegetables.

Italian Short Ribs with Parmesan Polenta

2	tablespoons vegetable oil
3	pounds bone-in beef short ribs, well trimmed, and cut into 3-inch pieces
1	teaspoon Italian seasoning
	Salt and black pepper, to taste
1½	cups chopped leeks (2 or 3 leeks)
1	cup white wine
¾	cup pitted kalamata or oil-cured olives
2	cups prepared pasta sauce
	Parmesan Polenta (recipe follows)

1 Heat oil in cooker over medium-high heat. Brown short ribs a few at a time; transfer to plate. Season with Italian seasoning, salt, and pepper.

2 Add leeks to cooker; cook and stir 2 minutes or until soft. Pour off any excess fat from cooker. Stir in wine, scraping up browned bits from bottom of cooker. Place ribs and olives in cooker. Pour pasta sauce over ribs.

3 Close cover securely. Place pressure regulator on vent pipe. Continue cooking over **high** heat until pressure regulator begins to rock. **Lower heat and cook 30 minutes with pressure regulator rocking slowly.**

4 **Remove from heat and let stand until cover lock drops.** Meanwhile, prepare Parmesan Polenta. Open cooker. Serve ribs and sauce with polenta.

Parmesan Polenta: Bring 2 cups water to a boil in large nonstick saucepan. Gradually whisk in 1 cup instant polenta until smooth and thick. Stir in ½ cup grated Parmesan cheese. Season with salt and pepper.

PRESTO
Tip

Polenta, an integral part of Northern Italian cuisine, is made from cornmeal. (Americans call this dish "mush.") If you'd like to make polenta from scratch, bring 3 cups water to a boil in a large nonstick saucepan over high heat. Slowly add 1 cup corn grits or yellow cornmeal, stirring constantly. Reduce heat to low; cook and stir until grits are tender, water is absorbed, and consistency is spoonable. Stir in ½ cup grated Parmesan cheese and 2 tablespoons butter. Season with salt and pepper. Leftover polenta can be cooled, then cut into slices and fried to serve as a side dish.

 A Bounty of Beef

Beef Pot Roast Dinner

makes 6 to 8 servings

1	teaspoon herbes de Provence*
1	teaspoon ground cumin
1	teaspoon ground sage
1	teaspoon black pepper
2	cloves garlic, minced
1	beef eye of round roast (about 2$^{1}/_{2}$ pounds), well trimmed
2	tablespoons olive oil
4	cups beef broth
4	small turnips, peeled and cut into wedges
12	medium-size fresh Brussels sprouts, trimmed
2	cups small new red potatoes, cut in half
2	cups baby carrots
1	cup pearl onions, skins removed, or 1 large onion, cut into wedges

Or substitute $^{1}/_{4}$ teaspoon each dried rosemary, thyme, sage, and savory.

1 Combine herbes de Provence, cumin, sage, pepper, and garlic in small bowl. Rub into all surfaces of beef.

2 Heat oil in cooker over medium-high heat. Brown beef evenly on all sides, about 4 minutes. Transfer beef from cooker to plate. Pour broth into cooker; stir, scraping up browned bits from bottom of cooker. Place beef on rack in cooker.

3 Close cover securely. Place pressure regulator on vent pipe. Continue cooking over **high** heat until pressure regulator begins to rock. **Lower heat and cook 35 minutes with pressure regulator rocking slowly.**

4 **Cool cooker at once under cold running water.** Open cooker. Add turnips, Brussels sprouts, potatoes, carrots, and onions to cooker. Close cover securely. Place pressure regulator on vent pipe. Continue cooking over **high** heat until pressure regulator begins to rock. **Lower heat and cook 3 minutes with pressure regulator rocking slowly.**

5 **Cool cooker at once under cold running water.** Remove beef and vegetables; arrange on serving platter. Serve with au jus or thicken sauce, if desired.

 A Bounty of Beef

Beef Pot Pie

makes 4 to 6 servings

1/2	package (about 15 ounces) refrigerated prepared pie crust (1 crust)
1/2	cup all-purpose flour
1	teaspoon salt, divided
1/2	teaspoon black pepper, divided
1 1/2	pounds lean beef stew meat, cut into 1-inch cubes
3	tablespoons olive oil, divided
1	cup beef broth
1/2	cup stout, dark beer, or ale
1	teaspoon chopped fresh thyme or 1/2 teaspoon dried thyme
1	pound new red potatoes, cubed
2	cups baby carrots, halved crosswise
1	cup frozen pearl onions, thawed, or 1 large onion, chopped
1	parsnip, peeled and cut into 1-inch pieces

1 Let pie crust stand at room temperature 15 minutes. Meanwhile, combine flour, 1/2 teaspoon salt, and 1/4 teaspoon pepper in large resealable plastic food storage bag. Add beef and toss to coat evenly; shake off excess flour mixture.

2 Heat 1 tablespoon oil in cooker over medium-high heat. Brown one-third of beef evenly on all sides. Transfer beef from cooker to plate; repeat with remaining oil and beef. Return all beef to cooker with any juices. Stir in broth, stout, thyme, remaining 1/2 teaspoon salt, and remaining 1/4 teaspoon pepper.

3 Close cover securely. Place pressure regulator on vent pipe. Cook over **high** heat until pressure regulator begins to rock. **Lower heat and cook 8 minutes with pressure regulator rocking slowly.**

4 **Cool cooker at once under cold running water.** Open cooker. Stir in potatoes, carrots, onions, and parsnip. Close cover securely. Place pressure regulator on vent pipe. Continue cooking over **high** heat until pressure regulator begins to rock. **Lower heat and cook 2 minutes with pressure regulator rocking slowly.**

5 **Cool cooker at once under cold running water.** Open cooker and adjust salt and pepper, to taste.

6 Heat oven to 425°F. Transfer beef filling to 2 1/2- to 3-quart casserole dish. Unfold and place pie crust over casserole; press edges to seal. Cut slits in crust to vent. Bake 15 to 20 minutes or until crust is golden brown. Cool slightly before serving.

Savory Beef Brisket

$^1/_2$	teaspoon salt
$^1/_2$	teaspoon black pepper
1	small beef brisket (2 to $2^1/_2$ pounds), well trimmed
1	cup beef or chicken broth
1	large onion, thinly sliced
$^2/_3$	cup prepared chili sauce
$1^1/_2$	tablespoons firmly packed brown sugar
$^1/_2$	teaspoon dried thyme
$^1/_4$	teaspoon ground cinnamon
2	large sweet potatoes, peeled and cut into 1-inch pieces
1	cup (5 ounces) pitted prunes, cut in half

1 Rub salt and pepper into all surfaces of beef. Pour broth into cooker. Place beef on rack in cooker. Place onion on top of beef.

2 Combine chili sauce, brown sugar, thyme, and cinnamon in small bowl. Pour over beef in cooker.

3 Close cover securely. Place pressure regulator on vent pipe. Cook over **high** heat until pressure regulator begins to rock. **Lower heat and cook 30 minutes with pressure regulator rocking slowly.**

4 **Remove from heat and let stand until cover lock drops.** Open cooker and remove beef. Cover loosely with aluminum foil to keep warm. Remove rack.

5 Add sweet potatoes and prunes to cooker. Close cover securely. Place pressure regulator on vent pipe. Cook over **high** heat until pressure regulator begins to rock. **Lower heat and cook 3 minutes with pressure regulator rocking slowly.**

6 **Cool cooker at once under cold running water.** Open cooker. Remove potatoes and prunes with slotted spoon. Simmer sauce, uncovered, to desired thickness. Slice brisket across the grain into thin slices. Serve with sauce, sweet potatoes, and prunes.

Beef Stew with a Coffee Kick

makes 6 servings

$1/3$	cup all-purpose flour
1	teaspoon salt
1	teaspoon dried marjoram
$1/2$	teaspoon garlic powder
$1/2$	teaspoon black pepper
2	pounds lean beef stew meat, cut into 1-inch cubes
3	to 4 tablespoons vegetable oil, divided
3	small onions, cut into wedges
1	cup strong brewed coffee, at room temperature
$1/2$	cup reduced-sodium beef broth
1	can ($14 1/2$ ounces) diced tomatoes, undrained
1	bay leaf
2	cups peeled cubed potatoes
4	stalks celery, cut into $1/2$-inch slices
4	medium carrots, cut into $1/2$-inch slices

1 Combine flour, salt, marjoram, garlic powder, and pepper in large bowl. Add beef and toss to coat all surfaces; shake off excess flour mixture. Heat 1 tablespoon oil in cooker over medium-high heat. Brown one-third of beef evenly on all sides. Transfer beef from cooker to plate; repeat with remaining oil and beef.

2 Add remaining 1 tablespoon oil to cooker, if necessary. Cook and stir onions over medium heat 2 minutes or until soft. Add coffee and broth; stir, scraping up browned bits from bottom of cooker. Place beef and any juices in cooker. Stir in tomatoes and bay leaf.

3 Close cover securely. Place pressure regulator on vent pipe. Continue cooking over **high** heat until pressure regulator begins to rock. **Lower heat and cook 8 minutes with pressure regulator rocking slowly.**

4 **Cool cooker at once under cold running water.** Open cooker. Stir in potatoes, celery, and carrots. Close cover securely. Place pressure regulator on vent pipe. Continue cooking over **high** heat until pressure regulator begins to rock. **Lower heat and cook 3 minutes with pressure regulator rocking slowly.**

5 **Cool cooker at once under cold running water.** Open cooker. Remove bay leaf before serving stew.

 A Bounty of Beef

Stuffed Flank Steak

1	large wide, thin beef flank steak (1$\frac{1}{2}$ to 2 pounds)
2	cups dry red wine, divided
$\frac{1}{4}$	cup soy sauce
2	cloves garlic, minced
$\frac{1}{2}$	teaspoon salt
$\frac{1}{2}$	teaspoon black pepper
$\frac{1}{4}$	teaspoon ground cumin
$\frac{1}{4}$	teaspoon dried thyme
1	cup frozen chopped spinach, thawed and squeezed dry
1	jar (7 ounces) roasted red bell peppers, drained and chopped
$\frac{1}{2}$	cup crumbled blue cheese
1	cup beef broth

1 Pound beef to even thickness, if necessary. Place in large resealable plastic food storage bag or glass dish. Combine 1 cup wine, soy sauce, garlic, salt, pepper, cumin, and thyme in small bowl; mix thoroughly. Pour marinade over beef. Refrigerate 2 to 4 hours or overnight.

2 Remove beef from marinade, reserving marinade. Pat dry and place on flat work surface. Combine spinach, roasted peppers, and cheese in medium bowl. Spoon mixture lengthwise on two-thirds of beef. Roll beef tightly around filling. Tie with kitchen twine, secure edges with toothpick, or wrap in cheesecloth.

3 Place rolled-up beef, reserved marinade, broth, and remaining 1 cup wine in cooker. Close cover securely. Place pressure regulator on vent pipe. Cook over **high** heat until pressure regulator begins to rock. **Lower heat and cook 20 minutes with pressure regulator rocking slowly.**

4 **Remove from heat and let stand until cover lock drops.** Open cooker and remove beef. Cover loosely with aluminum foil to keep warm; let stand 10 minutes. Remove twine before slicing. Meanwhile, simmer sauce to desired thickness.

Tex-Mex Chili

4	bacon slices, diced
2	pounds boneless beef top round or chuck shoulder steak, cut into $\frac{1}{2}$-inch cubes
1	medium onion, chopped
2	cloves garlic, minced
$2\frac{1}{4}$	cups water
$\frac{1}{4}$	cup chili powder
1	teaspoon dried oregano
1	teaspoon ground cumin
1	teaspoon salt
$\frac{1}{2}$	to 1 teaspoon ground red pepper
$\frac{1}{2}$	teaspoon hot pepper sauce
	Additional chopped onion (optional)

1 Fry bacon in cooker over medium-high heat until crisp. Remove bacon with slotted spoon to paper towels. Brown beef in bacon drippings in batches; transfer to plate.

2 Reduce heat to medium. Cook and stir onion and garlic in bacon drippings 2 minutes or until soft. Return beef and bacon to cooker. Add water, chili powder, oregano, cumin, salt, red pepper, and hot pepper sauce; stir to mix well.

3 Close cover securely. Place pressure regulator on vent pipe. Continue cooking over **high** heat until pressure regulator begins to rock. **Lower heat and cook 14 minutes with pressure regulator rocking slowly.**

4 **Remove from heat and let stand until cover lock drops.** Open cooker. Simmer, uncovered, to desired thickness, if necessary. Serve with additional chopped onion, if desired.

PRESTO
Tip

Texas chili doesn't contain any beans. But if you want to stretch this recipe and dilute some of the spiciness—and you don't live in Texas!—feel free to add some canned pinto beans to the chili in step 4.

Thyme-Scented Brisket Dinner

1	beef brisket (4 to 5 pounds), well trimmed
3¾	cups beef broth
2	large onions, thinly sliced
4	cloves garlic, minced
2	teaspoons dried thyme
1	teaspoon salt
½	teaspoon coriander
½	teaspoon black pepper
3	tablespoons cold water
2	tablespoons all-purpose flour
2	pounds red potatoes, quartered
1	pound baby carrots

1 Place beef, broth, onions, garlic, thyme, salt, coriander, and pepper in cooker. Close cover securely. Place pressure regulator on vent pipe. Cook over **high** heat until pressure regulator begins to rock. **Lower heat and cook 40 minutes with pressure regulator rocking slowly.**

2 **Cool cooker at once under cold running water.** Open cooker. Combine water and flour. Mix smooth and pour into cooker. Add potatoes and carrots. Close cover securely. Place pressure regulator on vent pipe. Continue cooking over **high** heat until pressure regulator begins to rock. **Lower heat and cook 3 minutes with pressure regulator rocking slowly.**

3 **Remove from heat and let stand until cover lock drops.** Open cooker and remove potatoes and carrots with slotted spoon; keep warm. Slice brisket across the grain into thin slices. Serve sauce over brisket and vegetables.

Saucy BBQ Short Ribs

2	cups regular cola (not diet) or beer
1	can (6 ounces) tomato paste
$^3/_4$	cup honey
$^1/_2$	cup cider vinegar
1	teaspoon salt
1	teaspoon black pepper
2	cloves garlic, minced
	Dash hot pepper sauce (optional)
4	pounds beef short ribs, well trimmed and cut into 2-inch lengths

1 Combine cola, tomato paste, honey, vinegar, salt, pepper, garlic, and hot pepper sauce, if desired, in cooker. Stir in short ribs, coating evenly with sauce.

2 Close cover securely. Place pressure regulator on vent pipe. Cook over **high** heat until pressure regulator begins to rock. **Lower heat and cook 25 minutes with pressure regulator rocking slowly.**

3 **Remove from heat and let stand until cover lock drops.** Open cooker. Serve sauce over ribs.

Spicy Beef Tacos

Filling

2	tablespoons vegetable oil, divided
1	pound boneless beef chuck, cut into 1-inch cubes
1	can (14$\frac{1}{2}$ ounces) diced tomatoes, undrained
1	teaspoon chili powder
1	clove garlic, minced
$\frac{1}{2}$	teaspoon ground cumin
$\frac{1}{4}$	teaspoon salt

Tacos

12	corn taco shells or flour tortillas, warmed
1	cup (4 ounces) shredded mild Cheddar cheese
2	to 3 cups shredded iceberg lettuce
1	large fresh tomato, seeded and chopped
	Fresh cilantro, coarsely chopped (optional)

1 Heat 1 tablespoon oil in cooker over medium-high heat. Brown one-half of beef evenly on all sides. Transfer beef from cooker to plate; repeat with remaining oil and beef. Return beef to cooker. Stir in diced tomatoes, chili powder, garlic, cumin, and salt.

2 Close cover securely. Place pressure regulator on vent pipe. Continue cooking over **high** heat until pressure regulator begins to rock. **Lower heat and cook 14 minutes with pressure regulator rocking slowly.**

3 **Remove from heat and let stand until cover lock drops.** Open cooker. Pull beef into coarse shreds using two forks. Cook, uncovered, 10 to 15 minutes over medium heat or until most of liquid has evaporated. Keep warm.

4 Assemble tacos; place beef in shells and garnish with cheese, lettuce, chopped tomato, and cilantro, if desired.

Pork, Lamb, and Veal

Italian Tomato-Braised Lamb

makes 4 servings

4	bone-in lamb shoulder chops (about 1 inch thick, about $2\frac{1}{2}$ pounds)
$1\frac{1}{2}$	teaspoons dried oregano
	Salt and black pepper, to taste
2	tablespoons olive oil
2	onions, cut into quarters and thinly sliced
3	cloves garlic, minced
1	can (28 ounces) whole plum tomatoes, undrained
$1\frac{3}{4}$	cups beef broth
2	tablespoons red wine vinegar
3	to 4 sprigs fresh rosemary
	Hot cooked polenta or pasta

1 Season both sides of lamb with oregano, salt, and pepper. Heat oil in cooker over medium heat. Cook and stir onions and garlic 3 minutes or until soft. Pour tomatoes, broth, and vinegar into cooker. Place lamb and rosemary in cooker.

2 Close cover securely. Place pressure regulator on vent pipe. Continue cooking over **high** heat until pressure regulator begins to rock. **Lower heat and cook 12 minutes with pressure regulator rocking slowly.**

3 **Cool cooker at once under cold running water.** Open cooker. Remove and discard rosemary sprigs. Remove chops; cover loosely with aluminum foil to keep warm. Bring sauce to a boil, uncovered, over high heat. Cook until thickened to desired consistency. Serve sauce with chops over polenta.

Honey Ginger Ribs

makes 4 servings

1	or 2 slabs baby back ribs (about 2 pounds)
4	medium green onions, chopped
1/2	cup hoisin sauce, divided*
3	tablespoons dry sherry or rice wine
2	tablespoons soy sauce
2	tablespoons honey
1	tablespoon cider vinegar
1	tablespoon firmly packed brown sugar
1	teaspoon minced fresh ginger
2	cloves garlic, minced
1/4	teaspoon Chinese five-spice powder**
1	cup chicken or beef broth
2	tablespoons cornstarch
	Sesame seeds (optional)

***Or substitute black bean sauce, kung pao sauce, or any flavor of prepared Asian sauce.**

****Chinese five-spice powder is a blend of cinnamon, cloves, fennel seed, anise, and Szechuan peppercorns. It's available in most supermarkets and at Asian grocery stores.**

1 Cut rib slabs into three or four pieces. Place in large resealable plastic food storage bag or glass dish. Combine green onions, 1/4 cup hoisin sauce, sherry, soy sauce, honey, vinegar, brown sugar, ginger, garlic, and five-spice powder in small bowl; mix thoroughly. Pour marinade over ribs. Refrigerate 2 to 4 hours or overnight, turning occasionally.

2 Pour broth into cooker. Add ribs and marinade. Close cover securely. Place pressure regulator on vent pipe. Cook over **high** heat until pressure regulator begins to rock. **Lower heat and cook 15 minutes with pressure regulator rocking slowly.**

3 **Cool cooker at once under cold running water.** Remove ribs; cover loosely with aluminum foil to keep warm. Skim excess fat from sauce. Combine 2 tablespoons sauce with cornstarch in small bowl; mix smooth. Add to sauce; cook and stir over medium-high heat until slightly thickened. Stir in remaining 1/4 cup hoisin sauce. Cook and stir until heated through. Brush sauce over ribs before serving. Sprinkle with sesame seeds, if desired.

Beer Barbecued Pulled Pork Sandwiches

1	tablespoon chili powder
1/2	teaspoon salt
1/4	teaspoon black pepper
2	pounds boneless pork shoulder roast, well trimmed, and cut into 3-inch pieces
1	tablespoon vegetable oil, divided
1	cup diced onions
1	bottle or can (12 ounces) ale or dark beer*
3/4	cup catsup
1/2	cup chicken broth
2	to 4 tablespoons honey
2	tablespoons cider vinegar
2	tablespoons whole-grain mustard
8	sandwich rolls
	Bread-and-butter pickle chips

For best flavor, do not use "light" beer.

1 Combine chili powder, salt, and pepper in small bowl. Sprinkle evenly over pork.

2 Heat 1 teaspoon oil in cooker over medium-high heat. Brown one-third of pork evenly on all sides. Transfer pork from cooker to plate; repeat with remaining oil and pork. Return all pork to cooker with any juices. Add onions, beer, catsup, broth, honey, vinegar, and mustard; stir to mix well.

3 Close cover securely. Place pressure regulator on vent pipe. Continue cooking over **high** heat until pressure regulator begins to rock. **Lower heat and cook 35 minutes with pressure regulator rocking slowly.**

4 **Remove from heat and let stand until cover lock drops.** Open cooker. Remove pork with slotted spoon. Shred with two forks into bite-sized pieces. Remove and discard any fat or connective tissue.

5 Bring sauce to a boil over medium-high heat. Cook and stir to desired thickness. Return pork to cooker; toss gently to coat evenly with sauce. Serve on rolls with pickle chips.

Beer-Braised Osso Bucco

makes 4 servings

$1/2$	cup all-purpose flour
1	teaspoon salt
$1/2$	teaspoon black pepper
4	veal shanks (about 3 pounds), cut into 1-inch rounds and tied with kitchen twine
4	tablespoons vegetable oil, divided
3	carrots, chopped
3	stalks celery, chopped
1	large onion, sliced
2	cloves garlic, minced
2	tablespoons tomato paste
1	bottle (12 ounces) beer
1	bay leaf
	Grated peel of 1 lemon

1 Combine flour, salt, and pepper in medium bowl. Coat all surfaces of shanks with flour mixture; shake off excess flour mixture.

2 Heat 1 tablespoon oil in cooker over medium-high heat. Brown one-third of shank pieces evenly on both sides, about 5 minutes. Transfer shanks from cooker to plate; repeat with remaining oil and shank pieces.

3 Heat remaining 1 tablespoon oil over medium heat. Add carrots, celery, onion, and garlic. Cook and stir 5 minutes or until soft. Stir in tomato paste until smooth. Add beer, scraping up browned bits from bottom of cooker. Place shanks and any juices in cooker. Stir in bay leaf and lemon peel.

4 Close cover securely. Place pressure regulator on vent pipe. Continue cooking over **high** heat until pressure regulator begins to rock. **Lower heat and cook 15 minutes with pressure regulator rocking slowly.**

5 **Remove from heat and let stand until cover lock drops.** Open cooker. Remove shanks; cover loosely with aluminum foil to keep warm. Remove and discard twine and bay leaf. Simmer sauce, uncovered, to desired thickness.

Shredded Chipotle Pork Tacos with Roasted Green Onions

makes 8 servings

1	boneless pork shoulder roast (about 2 pounds), well trimmed, and cut into 3-inch pieces
2	cups water
1	medium onion, thinly sliced
1/4	cup cider vinegar, divided
1	teaspoon salt
1	tablespoon olive oil
1	cup finely chopped onions
4	cloves garlic, minced
1	can (8 ounces) tomato sauce
3	chipotle peppers in adobo sauce, finely chopped and mashed with fork
1/2	teaspoon ground cumin
	Roasted Green Onions (recipe follows)
16	(6-inch) corn tortillas

1 Place pork, water, sliced onion, 3 tablespoons vinegar, and salt in cooker. Close cover securely. Place pressure regulator on vent pipe. Cook over **high** heat until pressure regulator begins to rock. **Lower heat and cook 35 minutes with pressure regulator rocking slowly.**

2 Remove from heat and let stand until cover lock drops. Open cooker. Remove pork and onions with slotted spoon. Shred pork with two forks; set aside. Reserve 1 cup cooking liquid; pour out remaining liquid from cooker. Wipe out cooker with paper towels, if necessary.

3 Heat oil in cooker over medium-high heat. Cook and stir chopped onions 3 minutes or until soft. Add garlic; cook and stir 15 seconds or until fragrant. Stir in tomato sauce, chipotles, cumin, remaining 1 tablespoon vinegar, shredded pork, sliced onion, and reserved 1 cup cooking liquid. Cook and stir 2 minutes or until heated through. Remove from heat; cover and let stand 10 minutes. Meanwhile, prepare Roasted Green Onions.

4 Heat tortillas over stovetop burner or grill about 15 seconds per side or until lightly charred. Fill evenly with pork mixture and Roasted Green Onions.

Roasted Green Onions: Preheat oven to 425°F. Trim 16 green onions; place on large baking sheet. Drizzle with 2 teaspoons olive oil; toss gently to coat. Arrange in single layer; bake 10 minutes. Sprinkle with salt.

Pork Loin in Chili-Spice Sauce

1	pork loin (about 1¹/₂ pounds), well trimmed
1¹/₂	cups orange juice, divided
1	cup chopped onion
2	cloves garlic, minced
1	tablespoon cider vinegar
1¹/₂	teaspoons chili powder
1	teaspoon salt
¹/₄	teaspoon dried thyme
¹/₄	teaspoon ground cumin
¹/₄	teaspoon ground cinnamon
¹/₈	teaspoon ground allspice
¹/₈	teaspoon ground cloves
2	tablespoons olive oil
	Fruit Chutney (recipe follows, optional)

1 Place pork in large resealable plastic food storage bag or glass dish. Combine ¹/₄ cup orange juice, onion, garlic, vinegar, chili powder, salt, thyme, cumin, cinnamon, allspice, and cloves in small bowl; mix thoroughly. Pour marinade over pork. Refrigerate 2 to 4 hours or overnight.

2 Remove pork from marinade, reserving marinade. Heat oil in cooker over medium heat. Brown pork evenly on all sides, about 6 minutes. Add remaining 1¹/₄ cups orange juice and reserved marinade to cooker.

3 Close cover securely. Place pressure regulator on vent pipe. Continue cooking over **high** heat until pressure regulator begins to rock. **Lower heat and cook 20 minutes with pressure regulator rocking slowly.**

4 **Remove from heat and let stand until cover lock drops.** Open cooker. Remove pork; cover loosely with aluminum foil to keep warm. Let stand 5 minutes before slicing. If desired, prepare Fruit Chutney. Or bring remaining liquid to a boil, uncovered, over high heat; cook until thickened to desired consistency. Serve with pork.

Fruit Chutney

- **¹⁄₄** cup apricot preserves or orange marmalade
- **1** mango, diced
- **¹⁄₂** cup diced fresh pineapple
- **2** green onions, minced
- **1** tablespoon minced red jalapeño or Fresno pepper*

Hot peppers can sting and irritate the skin, so wear rubber gloves when handling peppers and do not touch your eyes.

Add preserves to cooking liquid after removing pork. Cook and stir 10 minutes over medium-high heat until reduced by half. Add mango, pineapple, green onions, and jalapeño. Cook and stir 5 minutes or until heated through. Serve with pork.

Canton Pork Stew

1	cup chicken broth
1	tablespoon hoisin sauce
3	tablespoons soy sauce
1/4	cup dry sherry
1 1/2	tablespoons cornstarch
2	tablespoons vegetable oil, divided
1	boneless pork shoulder roast (about 1 1/2 pounds), well trimmed and cut into 1-inch pieces
1	large onion, diced
3	cloves garlic, minced
1	teaspoon five-spice powder*
1/2	teaspoon salt
2	cups baby carrots
1	large green bell pepper, cut into 1-inch pieces
	Finely chopped cilantro (optional)

Chinese five-spice powder is a blend of cinnamon, cloves, fennel seed, anise, and Szechuan peppercorns. It's available in most supermarkets and at Asian grocery stores.

1. Combine broth, hoisin sauce, soy sauce, and sherry in small bowl. Transfer 3 tablespoons broth mixture to cup. Add cornstarch to cup and mix until smooth; set aside.

2. Heat 1 tablespoon oil in cooker over medium-high heat. Brown one-half of pork evenly on all sides. Transfer pork from cooker to plate; repeat with remaining oil and pork.

3. Cook and stir onion 3 minutes or until soft. Add garlic, five-spice powder, and salt; cook and stir 30 seconds. Return all pork to cooker with any juices. Pour in broth mixture from bowl.

4. Close cover securely. Place pressure regulator on vent pipe. Continue cooking over **high** heat until pressure regulator begins to rock. **Lower heat and cook 13 minutes with pressure regulator rocking slowly.**

5 **Cool cooker at once under cold running water.** Open cooker. Add carrots and bell pepper. Close cover securely. Place pressure regulator on vent pipe. Continue cooking over **high** heat until pressure regulator begins to rock. **Lower heat and cook 2 minutes with pressure regulator rocking slowly.**

6 **Cool cooker at once under cold running water.** Open cooker. Stir cornstarch mixture in cup. Add to sauce and mix well. Cook and stir until thickened. Serve with cilantro, if desired.

Ale'd Pork and Sauerkraut

makes 6 to 8 servings

2	teaspoons ground paprika
1	teaspoon garlic powder
$1/2$	teaspoon salt
$1/4$	teaspoon black pepper
1	boneless pork shoulder or pork butt roast (about $3^1/_2$ pounds), well trimmed
$1^1/_2$	tablespoons vegetable oil
1	jar (32 ounces) sauerkraut, undrained
1	can (12 ounces) ale or dark beer
$1/2$	cup chicken broth
$1^1/_2$	tablespoons granulated sugar

1 Combine paprika, garlic powder, salt, and pepper in small bowl. Rub into all surfaces of pork.

2 Heat oil in cooker over medium-high heat. Brown pork evenly on all sides, about 7 minutes. Transfer pork from cooker to plate. Stir in sauerkraut, ale, broth, and sugar, scraping up browned bits from bottom of cooker. Place pork on top of mixture.

3 Close cover securely. Place pressure regulator on vent pipe. Continue cooking over **high** heat until pressure regulator begins to rock. **Lower heat and cook 55 minutes with pressure regulator rocking slowly.**

4 **Remove from heat and let stand until cover lock drops.** Open cooker. Remove pork; cover loosely with aluminum foil to keep warm. Let stand 5 minutes before slicing. Serve with sauerkraut and juices.

PRESTO *Tip*

Pork should be cooked to an internal temperature of at least 160°F. Use a meat thermometer to check the temperature after opening the cooker. If necessary, close the cover and continue cooking a few minutes longer.

Pork Loin with Apple, Onion, and Beer Marmalade

3	to 4 tablespoons vegetable oil
1	bone-in pork loin or boneless pork roast (about 3 pounds), well trimmed
2	medium onions, chopped
1	bottle or can (12 ounces) lager beer
2	apples, peeled and thinly sliced*
2	tablespoons packed light brown sugar
1	teaspoon ground ginger
1/2	teaspoon ground cinnamon
1/2	teaspoon black pepper
1/8	teaspoon ground red pepper

Braeburn apples work well with this recipe.

1 Heat oil in cooker over medium heat. Brown pork evenly on all sides, about 7 minutes. Transfer pork from cooker to plate.

2 Cook and stir onions 3 minutes or until lightly browned. Stir in beer, apples, brown sugar, ginger, cinnamon, black pepper, and red pepper. Place pork in cooker.

3 Close cover securely. Place pressure regulator on vent pipe. Continue cooking over **high** heat until pressure regulator begins to rock. **Lower heat and cook 30 minutes with pressure regulator rocking slowly.**

4 **Remove from heat and let stand until cover lock drops.** Open cooker. Remove pork; cover loosely with aluminum foil to keep warm. Let stand 5 minutes before slicing. Simmer marmalade, uncovered, stirring occasionally, to desired thickness. Serve with pork.

PRESTO *Tip*

Pork should be cooked to an internal temperature of at least 160°F. Use a meat thermometer to check the temperature after opening the cooker. If necessary, close the cover and continue cooking a few minutes longer.

Pork Roast with Tart Cherries

1	tablespoon plus 1 teaspoon prepared grated horseradish, divided
2	teaspoons ground coriander
1/2	teaspoon black pepper
1	tablespoon olive oil
1	boneless pork loin roast (about 2 pounds), well trimmed
1	can (about 14 ounces) pitted tart cherries, undrained
1/2	cup chicken broth
1/4	cup Madeira wine, dry sherry, or white wine
4	teaspoons grated orange peel
1	tablespoon brown sugar
1	tablespoon Dijon mustard
1/8	teaspoon ground cloves
	Orange slices (optional)

1 Combine 1 tablespoon horseradish, coriander, and pepper in small bowl; set aside.

2 Heat oil in cooker over medium heat. Brown pork roast evenly on all sides, about 6 minutes. Transfer pork from cooker to plate. Rub horseradish mixture evenly over pork.

3 Combine cherries, broth, and wine in cooker. Place pork on rack in cooker. Close cover securely. Place pressure regulator on vent pipe. Continue cooking over **high** heat until pressure regulator begins to rock. **Lower heat and cook 30 minutes with pressure regulator rocking slowly.**

4 **Remove from heat and let stand until cover lock drops.** Open cooker. Remove pork; cover loosely with aluminum foil to keep warm. Remove rack.

5 Strain sauce, reserving cherries. Return sauce to cooker. Stir in orange peel, brown sugar, mustard, remaining 1 teaspoon horseradish, and cloves. Bring to a boil over medium-high heat. Cook and stir 10 minutes or until slightly thickened. Stir in reserved cherries. Serve sauce with pork. Garnish with orange slices, if desired.

PRESTO *Tip* **If you like spicier food, double the amount of the horseradish, coriander, and pepper used for the rub.**

Greek-Style Braised Lamb Chops

3	cloves garlic, minced
1	teaspoon Greek seasoning
1	teaspoon salt
1	teaspoon black pepper
4	bone-in lamb shoulder chops (about 1 inch thick, about $2\frac{1}{2}$ pounds)
3	tablespoons olive oil
1	large onion, sliced
$2\frac{1}{4}$	cups beer
3	plum tomatoes, cut into 6 wedges
$\frac{1}{2}$	cup pitted kalamata olives
1	tablespoon chopped fresh parsley

1 Combine garlic, seasoning, salt, and pepper in small bowl. Rub into both sides of lamb chops.

2 Heat oil in cooker over medium heat. Brown lamb evenly on both sides, about 3 minutes. Transfer lamb from cooker to plate. Cook and stir onion 3 minutes or until soft. Pour beer into cooker. Place lamb, tomatoes, and olives in cooker.

3 Close cover securely. Place pressure regulator on vent pipe. Continue cooking over **high** heat until pressure regulator begins to rock. **Lower heat and cook 12 minutes with pressure regulator rocking slowly.**

4 **Cool cooker at once under cold running water.** Open cooker. Remove lamb. Remove vegetables with slotted spoon. Cover lamb and vegetables loosely with aluminum foil to keep warm. Bring remaining liquid to a boil, uncovered, over high heat. Cook and stir until thickened to desired consistency. Serve sauce over chops and vegetables. Sprinkle evenly with parsley.

PRESTO
Tip

To make your own Greek seasoning, combine $1\frac{1}{2}$ teaspoons dried oregano, 1 teaspoon dried mint, 1 teaspoon dried thyme, $\frac{1}{2}$ teaspoon dried basil, $\frac{1}{2}$ teaspoon dried marjoram, $\frac{1}{4}$ teaspoon onion powder, and $\frac{1}{4}$ teaspoon garlic powder in a small bowl. Store the seasoning in an airtight container.

Puerco Sabrosas (Savory Pork)

Rice

1	cup long-grain white rice
3¹/₂	cups water, divided
¹/₂	teaspoon salt

Pork

3	tablespoons vegetable oil, divided
1	boneless pork shoulder roast (about 1¹/₂ pounds), well trimmed, and cut into thin strips
1	medium onion, chopped
1	green bell pepper, chopped
2	green chiles (Hatch or Anaheim), seeded and minced
1	clove garlic, minced
1	can (14¹/₂ ounces) whole stewed tomatoes, crushed
¹/₂	cup water
2	tablespoons chopped fresh cilantro
1	teaspoon chopped fresh oregano
1	teaspoon ground cumin
	Salt and black pepper, to taste

1 Combine rice, 1¹/₂ cups water, and ¹/₂ teaspoon salt in metal bowl that fits loosely in cooker. Cover bowl firmly with aluminum foil. Pour 2 cups water into cooker. Using foil lifting handle, place bowl on rack in cooker, folding handle ends down over bowl (see page 7).

2 Close cover securely. Place pressure regulator on vent pipe. Cook over **high** heat until pressure regulator begins to rock. **Lower heat and cook 5 minutes with pressure regulator rocking slowly.**

3 **Remove from heat and let stand until cover lock drops.** Open cooker. Use lifting handle to carefully remove bowl from cooker. Set rice aside; keep warm. Remove rack and drain water from cooker.

4 Heat 1 tablespoon oil in cooker over medium-high heat. Brown one-half of pork evenly on all sides. Transfer pork from cooker to plate; repeat with remaining oil and pork. Pour off excess fat from cooker.

5 Heat remaining 1 tablespoon oil in cooker over medium-high heat. Add onion, bell pepper, chiles, and garlic. Cook and stir 3 minutes or until soft. Stir in pork, tomatoes, $^1/_2$ cup water, cilantro, oregano, and cumin.

6 Close cover securely. Place pressure regulator on vent pipe. Continue cooking over **high** heat until pressure regulator begins to rock. **Lower heat and cook 15 minutes with pressure regulator rocking slowly.**

7 **Remove from heat and let stand until cover lock drops.** Open cooker. Season with salt and black pepper. Fluff rice gently with fork before serving with pork.

Chicken and Turkey

Braised Chicken with Vegetables

makes 2 to 4 servings

2	cups chicken broth
2	tablespoons lemon juice
$1\frac{1}{2}$	tablespoons salt-free seasoning blend
2	cloves garlic, minced
$\frac{3}{4}$	teaspoon cornstarch
$\frac{1}{2}$	teaspoon dried rosemary
$\frac{1}{2}$	teaspoon paprika
4	bone-in skinless chicken drumsticks
3	cups assorted chopped vegetables (cut yellow squash and zucchini into 1-inch cubes; cut carrots, onions, and bell peppers into $\frac{1}{2}$-inch slices)

Salt and black pepper, to taste

1 Combine broth, lemon juice, seasoning blend, garlic, cornstarch, rosemary, and paprika in cooker; stir to mix well. Add chicken.

2 Close cover securely. Place pressure regulator on vent pipe. Cook over **high** heat until pressure regulator begins to rock. **Lower heat and cook 8 minutes with pressure regulator rocking slowly.**

3 **Cool cooker at once under cold running water.** Open cooker and add vegetables. Close cover securely. Place pressure regulator on vent pipe. Continue cooking over **high** heat until pressure regulator begins to rock. **Lower heat and cook 1 minute with pressure regulator rocking slowly.**

4 **Cool cooker at once under cold running water.** Open cooker. Season with salt and pepper. Serve sauce over chicken and vegetables.

Lemon Rosemary Chicken and Potatoes

makes 4 servings

4	bone-in skinless chicken breast halves (about 6 ounces each)
2	pounds small red potatoes, cut into quarters
1	large onion, cut into 2-inch chunks
$\frac{1}{2}$	cup freshly squeezed lemon juice
6	tablespoons olive oil
6	cloves garlic, minced
2	tablespoons plus 1 teaspoon finely chopped fresh rosemary leaves or $2\frac{1}{4}$ teaspoons dried rosemary
2	teaspoons grated lemon peel
1	teaspoon salt
$\frac{1}{4}$	teaspoon black pepper
1	tablespoon vegetable oil
1	cup chicken stock or broth

1 Place chicken in large resealable plastic food storage bag or glass dish. Place potatoes and onion in another resealable bag or dish. Combine lemon juice, olive oil, garlic, rosemary, lemon peel, salt, and pepper in small bowl; mix thoroughly. Pour half of marinade over chicken; pour remaining marinade over potatoes and onion. Refrigerate 2 hours or overnight.

2 Remove chicken from marinade; discard marinade. Heat vegetable oil in cooker over medium heat. Brown chicken on all sides, 4 to 5 minutes. Transfer chicken from cooker to plate.

3 Remove potatoes and onion from marinade; reserve marinade. Cook and stir potatoes and onion until lightly browned. Remove from cooker. Place cooking rack in cooker. Place chicken, potatoes and onion, chicken stock, and reserved marinade in cooker.

4 Close cover securely. Place pressure regulator on vent pipe. Continue cooking over **high** heat until pressure regulator begins to rock. **Lower heat and cook 5 minutes with pressure regulator rocking slowly.**

5 **Cool cooker at once under cold running water.** Remove chicken and vegetables with slotted spoon; keep warm. Skim any fat from cooking liquid. Cook, uncovered, over medium-high heat until desired thickness. Serve sauce over chicken and vegetables.

Spanish Braised Chicken with Green Olives and Rice

2	pounds bone-in skinless chicken thighs (about 6 thighs)
³/₄	cup dry sherry
1¹/₂	teaspoons dried sage
1	teaspoon ground paprika
2	cups long-grain white rice
4¹/₄	cups chicken broth, divided
3³/₄	cups water, divided
2	tablespoons olive oil
1	packet coriander and annatto seasoning*
¹/₂	teaspoon salt
2	tablespoons vegetable oil
³/₄	cup pimiento-stuffed green olives

Or combine ¹/₃ teaspoon ground coriander, ¹/₃ teaspoon ground cumin, ¹/₃ teaspoon ground annatto seeds or ground paprika, ¹/₃ teaspoon garlic powder, and ¹/₄ teaspoon salt.

1 Place chicken in large resealable plastic food storage bag or glass dish. Combine sherry, sage, and paprika in small bowl; mix thoroughly. Pour marinade over chicken. Refrigerate 2 to 4 hours.

2 Combine rice, 2 cups broth, 1³/₄ cups water, olive oil, seasoning, and salt in metal bowl that fits loosely in cooker. Cover bowl firmly with aluminum foil. Pour remaining 2 cups water into cooker. Using foil lifting handle, place bowl on rack in cooker, folding handle ends down over bowl (see page 7).

3 Close cover securely. Place pressure regulator on vent pipe. Cook over **high** heat until pressure regulator begins to rock. **Lower heat and cook 8 minutes with pressure regulator rocking slowly.**

4 **Remove from heat and let stand until cover lock drops.** Open cooker. Use lifting handle to carefully remove bowl from cooker. Set rice aside; keep warm. Remove rack; drain water from cooker.

5 Remove chicken from marinade; reserve marinade. Heat vegetable oil in cooker over medium heat and brown chicken on both sides, 3 to 4 minutes. Add remaining 2¹/₄ cups broth, reserved marinade, and olives.

6 Close cover securely. Place pressure regulator on vent pipe. Continue cooking over **high** heat until pressure regulator begins to rock. **Lower heat and cook 8 minutes with pressure regulator rocking slowly.**

7 **Cool cooker at once under cold running water.** Fluff rice gently with fork before serving with chicken and sauce.

Chili Turkey Breast with Cilantro-Lime Rice

Turkey

$1\frac{1}{2}$	tablespoons chili powder
2	teaspoons dried oregano
$1\frac{1}{2}$	teaspoons ground cumin
$\frac{1}{2}$	teaspoon red pepper flakes
$\frac{1}{2}$	teaspoon salt
$\frac{1}{2}$	teaspoon black pepper
1	bone-in turkey breast (about 4 pounds), skin removed
2	cups chicken broth

Rice

$4\frac{1}{2}$	cups water, divided
$1\frac{1}{2}$	cups long-grain white rice
2	medium red bell peppers, chopped
1	cup chopped green onions
$\frac{1}{2}$	cup chopped fresh cilantro
3	tablespoons olive oil
2	to 3 tablespoons lime juice
1	tablespoon grated lime peel
$\frac{3}{4}$	teaspoon salt
$\frac{1}{2}$	teaspoon ground turmeric (optional)

1 Combine chili powder, oregano, cumin, red pepper, salt, and black pepper in small bowl; mix thoroughly. Rub into all surfaces of turkey. Pour broth into cooker. Place turkey on rack in cooker.

2 Close cover securely. Place pressure regulator on vent pipe. Cook over **high** heat until pressure regulator begins to rock. **Lower heat and cook 35 minutes with pressure regulator rocking slowly.**

3 **Remove from heat and let stand until cover lock drops.** Open cooker. Remove turkey from cooker. Cover loosely with aluminum foil to keep warm. Transfer broth to medium bowl; cool and reserve for another use.

4 Combine 2¹/₂ cups water, rice, bell peppers, green onions, cilantro, oil, lime juice, lime peel, salt, and turmeric, if desired, in metal bowl that fits loosely in cooker. Cover bowl firmly with aluminum foil. Pour remaining 2 cups water into cooker. Using foil lifting handle, place bowl on rack in cooker, folding handle ends down over bowl (see page 7).

5 Close cover securely. Place pressure regulator on vent pipe. Cook over **high** heat until pressure regulator begins to rock. **Lower heat and cook 5 minutes with pressure regulator rocking slowly.**

6 **Remove from heat and let stand until cover lock drops.** Use lifting handle to carefully remove bowl from cooker; remove foil. Fluff rice gently with fork before serving with turkey.

Chile Verde Chicken Stew

3	tablespoons vegetable oil, divided
2	onions, chopped
2	cloves garlic, chopped
1	pound tomatillos (about 9), husked and cut in half
2	cups reduced-sodium chicken broth
2	cans (4 ounces each) mild green chiles
1	tablespoon dried oregano
1	tablespoon ground cumin
1	teaspoon granulated sugar
1	teaspoon salt, divided
$1/3$	cup all-purpose flour
$1/4$	teaspoon black pepper
$1^1/2$	pounds boneless skinless chicken breasts, cut into $1^1/2$-inch pieces
5	red potatoes (about 1 pound), diced

Chopped fresh cilantro, sour cream, shredded Monterey Jack cheese, lime wedges, diced avocado, hot pepper sauce (optional)

1 Heat 1 tablespoon oil in cooker over medium heat. Cook and stir onions 3 minutes or until soft. Stir in garlic; cook 30 seconds. Stir in tomatillos, broth, chiles, oregano, cumin, sugar, and $1/2$ teaspoon salt.

2 Close cover securely. Place pressure regulator on vent pipe. Continue cooking over **high** heat until pressure regulator begins to rock. **Lower heat and cook 3 minutes with pressure regulator rocking slowly.**

3 **Cool cooker at once under cold running water.** Open cooker. Carefully process tomatillo mixture in 2-cup batches in blender or food processor until almost smooth. Pour into large bowl; set aside. Wipe out cooker with paper towels, if necessary.

4 Combine flour, remaining $1/2$ teaspoon salt, and pepper in large bowl. Add chicken and toss to coat all surfaces. Heat 1 tablespoon oil in cooker over medium-high heat. Lightly brown one-half of chicken on all sides. Transfer from cooker to plate. Repeat with remaining oil and chicken. Return all chicken to cooker. Add tomatillo mixture and stir, scraping up browned bits from bottom of cooker. Stir in potatoes.

5 Close cover securely. Place pressure regulator on vent pipe. Cook over **high** heat until pressure regulator begins to rock. **Lower heat and cook 5 minutes with pressure regulator rocking slowly.**

6 **Cool cooker at once under cold running water.** Open cooker. Serve immediately with desired toppings.

Tuscan Chicken Breasts

Polenta (recipe follows, optional)

$1/2$	**teaspoon garlic powder**
$1/2$	**teaspoon Italian seasoning**
$1/4$	**teaspoon salt**
$3/4$	**teaspoon black pepper, divided**
8	**boneless skinless chicken breasts (about 3 pounds)**
1	**tablespoon vegetable oil, divided**
$1/2$	**cup chopped onion**
2	**cloves garlic, minced**
8	**plum tomatoes, coarsely chopped**
1	**can (8 ounces) tomato sauce**
2	**teaspoons dried basil**
2	**teaspoons dried oregano**
2	**teaspoons dried rosemary, crushed**

1 Prepare and refrigerate polenta up to a day in advance, if desired.

2 Combine garlic powder, Italian seasoning, salt, and $1/4$ teaspoon pepper in small bowl. Rub into all surfaces of chicken. Heat 1 teaspoon oil in cooker over medium heat. Brown one-third of chicken lightly on both sides. Transfer chicken from cooker to plate. Repeat with remaining oil and chicken.

3 Add onion; cook and stir 2 to 3 minutes or until lightly browned. Add garlic; cook and stir 15 seconds or until fragrant. Add tomatoes, tomato sauce, basil, oregano, rosemary, and remaining $1/2$ teaspoon pepper; stir to mix well. Place chicken on sauce.

4 Close cover securely. Place pressure regulator on vent pipe. Continue cooking over **high** heat until pressure regulator begins to rock. **Lower heat and cook 4 minutes with pressure regulator rocking slowly.**

5 **Remove from heat and let stand until cover lock drops.** Open cooker. Serve chicken with sauce and polenta slices, if desired.

Polenta: Bring 4 cups chicken broth to a boil in large saucepan over high heat. Slowly stir in 1 cup polenta or yellow cornmeal. Reduce heat to low; cook 15 to 20 minutes, stirring frequently, or until very thick. (Mixture may be lumpy.) Pour polenta into greased 9×5-inch loaf pan. Cool; cover and refrigerate 2 to 3 hours or until firm. To serve, remove polenta from pan. Cut crosswise into 16 slices. Cut slices into triangles, if desired. Coat large nonstick skillet with nonstick cooking spray; heat over medium heat. Cook polenta about 4 minutes per side or until lightly browned. Serve warm.

Dijon Chicken

6	boneless skinless chicken breasts
¾	cup vinaigrette or balsamic vinaigrette salad dressing
½	cup Dijon mustard
¼	cup firmly packed brown sugar
4	teaspoons vegetable oil, divided
½	cup chicken broth
	Salt and black pepper, to taste

1 Place chicken in large resealable plastic food storage bag or glass dish. Combine salad dressing, mustard, and brown sugar in small bowl; mix well. Pour marinade over chicken. Refrigerate 3 to 4 hours.

2 Remove chicken from marinade, reserving marinade. Heat 2 teaspoons oil in cooker over medium heat. Brown one-half of chicken on both sides. Transfer chicken from cooker to plate. Repeat with remaining oil and chicken. Return all chicken to cooker. Add broth and reserved marinade.

3 Close cover securely. Place pressure regulator on vent pipe. Continue cooking over **high** heat until pressure regulator begins to rock. **Lower heat and cook 4 minutes with pressure regulator rocking slowly.**

4 **Cool cooker at once under cold running water.** Open cooker. Season with salt and pepper. Serve immediately.

Caramelized Lemongrass Chicken

2	stalks lemongrass
1½	pounds bone-in skinless chicken thighs (4 to 6 thighs)
¼	cup granulated sugar
3	tablespoons prepared fish sauce
1	tablespoon lemon juice
2	cloves garlic, slivered
¼	teaspoon black pepper
1	to 2 tablespoons vegetable oil
1	cup chicken broth

1 Remove outer leaves from lemongrass and discard. Trim off and discard upper stalks. Flatten lemongrass with meat mallet. Cut lemongrass into 1-inch pieces.

2 Place chicken in large resealable plastic food storage bag or glass dish. Combine lemongrass, sugar, fish sauce, lemon juice, garlic, and pepper in small bowl; mix thoroughly. Pour marinade over chicken. Refrigerate 1 to 4 hours.

3 Remove chicken from marinade; reserve marinade. Heat oil in cooker over medium heat. Brown chicken on both sides, about 4 minutes. Add broth and reserved marinade.

4 Close cover securely. Place pressure regulator on vent pipe. Continue cooking over **high** heat until pressure regulator begins to rock. **Lower heat and cook 8 minutes with pressure regulator rocking slowly.**

5 **Cool cooker at once under cold running water.** Open cooker. Serve immediately.

Spinach-Stuffed Chicken Breasts

5	ounces frozen chopped spinach, thawed and squeezed dry
1/4	cup grated Parmesan cheese
1	teaspoon grated lemon peel
1/8	teaspoon white or black pepper
1	cup thinly sliced mushrooms
4	boneless skinless chicken breasts (about 1 pound), well trimmed
6	slices (2 ounces) thinly sliced ham or turkey ham
	Ground paprika (optional)
1	cup white wine or white grape juice
2	tablespoons cold water
1	tablespoon cornstarch

1 Pat spinach dry with paper towels. Combine spinach, Parmesan, lemon peel, and pepper in medium bowl; set aside. Coat small nonstick skillet with nonstick cooking spray; add mushrooms. Cook and stir over medium heat 3 to 4 minutes or until tender; set aside.

2 Place each chicken breast between two sheets of plastic wrap or in large resealable plastic food storage bag. Pound with meat mallet until chicken is about 1/4 inch thick.

3 Arrange 1 1/2 slices ham over each chicken breast. Spread each with one-fourth of spinach mixture. Top each with one-fourth of mushrooms. Beginning with longer side, roll chicken tightly. Tie with kitchen twine or secure edges with toothpick. Sprinkle chicken with paprika, if desired. Pour wine into cooker. Place stuffed chicken, seam side down, in cooker.

4 Close cover securely. Place pressure regulator on vent pipe. Cook over **high** heat until pressure regulator begins to rock. **Lower heat and cook 10 minutes with pressure regulator rocking slowly.**

5 **Cool cooker at once under cold running water.** Open cooker. Remove chicken with slotted spoon; let stand 5 minutes. Combine water and cornstarch; add to sauce. Cook and stir sauce, uncovered, to desired thickness. Remove twine or toothpicks from chicken. Cut chicken into 1-inch slices with sharp knife, using gentle sawing motion for clean cuts. Serve sauce over chicken.

Chicken Cacciatore

1	chicken (about 3 pounds), cut up
1½	cups sliced onions
1	cup diced tomatoes
½	cup chopped carrots
½	cup chopped celery
⅓	cup white wine
2	cloves garlic, minced
2	tablespoons minced fresh parsley
1	teaspoon dried oregano
1	teaspoon salt
¼	teaspoon black pepper
1	can (6 ounces) tomato paste

1 Place chicken, onions, tomatoes, carrots, celery, wine, garlic, parsley, oregano, salt, and pepper in cooker.

2 Close cover securely. Place pressure regulator on vent pipe. Cook over **high** heat until pressure regulator begins to rock. **Lower heat and cook 8 minutes with pressure regulator rocking slowly.**

3 **Cool cooker at once under cold running water.** Open cooker. Remove chicken; keep warm. Add tomato paste to cooker; stir to mix well. Simmer, uncovered, until sauce thickens. Serve sauce over chicken.

PRESTO

Tip

Although this recipe calls for white wine, in Italy, this dish is also prepared with red wine. Also, don't be afraid to use a less-dry wine if that's all you have on hand. The slight sweetness can tone down the acidity of the tomato paste.

Mustard, Garlic, and Herb Roasted Turkey Breast

1	tablespoon vegetable oil
1	bone-in turkey breast (about 3 pounds), skin removed
2	tablespoons spicy brown mustard
2	tablespoons chopped fresh parsley
1	tablespoon chopped fresh thyme or 1 teaspoon dried thyme
1	tablespoon chopped fresh sage or 1 teaspoon dried sage
1	clove garlic, minced
$\frac{1}{2}$	teaspoon black pepper
$\frac{1}{4}$	teaspoon salt
$1\frac{1}{2}$	cups water

1 Heat oil in cooker over medium heat. Brown turkey evenly on all sides, 5 to 7 minutes. Remove turkey from cooker; remove cooker from heat.

2 Combine mustard, parsley, thyme, sage, garlic, pepper, and salt in small bowl; mix well. Rub mixture evenly over turkey. Pour water into cooker. Place turkey on rack in cooker.

3 Close cover securely. Place pressure regulator on vent pipe. Cook over **high** heat until pressure regulator begins to rock. **Lower heat and cook 35 minutes with pressure regulator rocking slowly.**

4 **Remove from heat and let stand until cover lock drops.** Open cooker. Transfer turkey to cutting board. Tent with aluminum foil to keep warm; let stand 10 minutes before slicing.

Beans *and* Rice

Pesto Rice and Beans

makes 4 servings

¹⁄₂	cup dried Great Northern beans
4	cups water, divided
2³⁄₄	cups chicken broth
¹⁄₂	cup white rice
4	ounces fresh green beans, cut into 1-inch pieces (³⁄₄ cup)
4	to 5 tablespoons prepared pesto
	Salt, to taste
	Shredded or grated Parmesan cheese, chopped plum tomatoes, chopped parsley (optional)

1 Rinse dried beans thoroughly in colander under cold running water, picking out any debris or blemished beans. Combine beans and 2 cups water. Soak 6 to 8 hours or overnight. After soaking, rinse and drain beans, and remove any loose skins.

2 Combine soaked beans, broth, and rice in metal bowl that fits loosely in cooker. Cover bowl firmly with aluminum foil. Pour 2 cups water into cooker. Using foil lifting handle, place bowl on rack in cooker, folding handle ends down over bowl (see page 7).

3 Close cover securely. Place pressure regulator on vent pipe. Cook over **high** heat until pressure regulator begins to rock. **Lower heat and cook 7 minutes with pressure regulator rocking slowly.**

4 Meanwhile, steam green beans in small saucepan 7 minutes or until tender. Drain; set aside.

5 **Cool cooker at once under cold running water.** Open cooker. Use lifting handle to carefully remove bowl from cooker; remove foil. Transfer rice and beans to large bowl. Stir in reserved green beans and pesto. Season with salt. Stir in Parmesan, tomatoes, and/or parsley, if desired.

Paella Salad

1½	cups chicken broth
1	cup brown rice
¼	teaspoon ground turmeric
2	cups water
1	jar (6 ounces) marinated artichokes, drained and marinade liquid reserved
1	tablespoon minced onion
¼	teaspoon dried oregano
1	cup small peeled and deveined cooked shrimp
½	cup frozen peas, thawed
2	ounces pepperoni, cut into thin julienne strips
1	jar (2 ounces) diced pimientos, drained
	Salt and black pepper, to taste
	Butter lettuce leaves (optional)

1 Combine broth, rice, and turmeric in metal bowl that fits loosely in cooker. Cover bowl firmly with aluminum foil. Pour water into cooker. Using foil lifting handle, place bowl on rack in cooker, folding handle ends down over bowl (see page 7).

2 Close cover securely. Place pressure regulator on vent pipe. Cook over **high** heat until pressure regulator begins to rock. **Lower heat and cook 10 minutes with pressure regulator rocking slowly.**

3 **Remove from heat and let stand until cover lock drops.** Open cooker. Use lifting handle to carefully remove bowl from cooker; remove foil. Transfer rice to large bowl. Stir in reserved artichoke marinade, onion, and oregano. Fluff with fork. Refrigerate 20 minutes or until cool.

4 Stir artichoke hearts, shrimp, peas, pepperoni, and pimientos into rice mixture. Season with salt and pepper. If desired, place lettuce leaves on plates before serving salad.

PRESTO
Tip

The rice absorbs the dressing upon standing. If you make the salad 24 hours before serving it, stir in a mixture of 1 tablespoon olive oil and ½ tablespoon white wine vinegar to perk up the flavor.

Four-Bean Chili Stew

3/4	cup dried kidney beans
3/4	cup dried chickpeas
3/4	cup dried Great Northern beans
3/4	cup dried black beans
11	cups water, divided
1	can (23 ounces) tomatillos
1	can (15 ounces) tomato sauce
1	cup prepared barbecue sauce
1	onion, chopped
1	zucchini, cut in half and then in 1-inch slices
1/2	red bell pepper, chopped
3	cloves garlic, minced
1 1/2	teaspoons ground cumin
1 1/2	teaspoons chili powder
1/2	teaspoon salt
1/4	teaspoon ground red pepper
	Flour tortillas, warmed (optional)
	Sour cream, chopped tomato, chopped onion, shredded Cheddar cheese, chopped fresh cilantro (optional)

1 Rinse beans separately in colander under cold running water, picking out any debris or blemished beans. Combine kidney beans, chickpeas, Great Northern beans, and 7 cups water in large bowl. Combine black beans and 2 1/2 cups water in medium bowl.* Soak 4 to 8 hours or overnight. After soaking, rinse and drain beans, and remove any loose skins.

2 Place all beans in cooker. Add remaining 1 1/2 cups water, tomatillos, tomato sauce, barbecue sauce, onion, zucchini, bell pepper, garlic, cumin, chili powder, salt, and red pepper; stir to mix well.

3 Close cover securely. Place pressure regulator on vent pipe. Cook over **high** heat until pressure regulator begins to rock. **Lower heat and cook 10 minutes with pressure regulator rocking slowly.**

4 **Remove from heat and let stand until cover lock drops.** Open cooker. Serve with tortillas and desired garnishes.

Soaking black beans with the other beans will turn the Great Northerns and chickpeas purple.

Vegetable Risotto

2	cups fat-free reduced-sodium chicken broth
1	cup arborio rice
$\frac{1}{2}$	cup diced onions
$\frac{1}{2}$	cup sliced carrots
$\frac{1}{4}$	cup white wine
1	portobello mushroom, chopped
2	teaspoons butter
2	cloves garlic, minced
$\frac{1}{2}$	teaspoon salt
2	cups water
$1\frac{1}{2}$	cups sliced asparagus
2	teaspoons freshly grated lemon peel
	Pinch each salt, black pepper, thyme, and minced fresh rosemary leaves

1 Combine broth, rice, onions, carrots, wine, mushroom, butter, garlic, and salt in metal bowl that fits loosely in cooker. Cover bowl firmly with aluminum foil. Pour water into cooker. Using foil lifting handle, place bowl on rack in cooker, folding handle ends down over bowl (see page 7).

2 Close cover securely. Place pressure regulator on vent pipe. Cook over **high** heat until pressure regulator begins to rock. **Lower heat and cook 5 minutes with pressure regulator rocking slowly.**

3 **Remove from heat and let stand until cover lock drops.** Open cooker. Use lifting handle to carefully remove bowl from cooker; remove foil. Stir in asparagus. Cover bowl firmly with aluminum foil. Return to cooker, using foil lifting handle and folding handle ends down over bowl.

4 Close cover securely. Place pressure regulator on vent pipe. **Cook over high heat only until pressure regulator begins to rock (0 minutes).**

5 **Cool cooker at once under cold running water.** Open cooker. Use lifting handle to carefully remove bowl from cooker; remove foil. Stir in lemon peel, salt, pepper, thyme, and rosemary. Serve immediately.

Fruited Rice

makes 6 servings

4	**cups water, divided**
¹⁄₂	**cup wild rice**
¹⁄₂	**cup brown rice**
3	**tablespoons minced fresh parsley**
2	**tablespoons minced onion**
1	**tablespoon butter**
2	**teaspoons packed brown sugar**
¹⁄₂	**teaspoon dried thyme**
¹⁄₄	**teaspoon ground black pepper**
¹⁄₈	**teaspoon ground red pepper**
¹⁄₄	**cup orange juice**
¹⁄₄	**cup chopped apricots**
¹⁄₄	**cup dried cranberries or cherries**
¹⁄₄	**cup raisins or currants**

PRESTO *Tip*

For faster preparation, omit wild rice. Instead, use 1 cup brown rice and 1¹⁄₂ cups water, and prepare the rice as directed in steps 3 to 5.

1 Combine ³⁄₄ cup water and wild rice in metal bowl that fits loosely in cooker. Cover bowl firmly with aluminum foil. Pour 2 cups water into cooker. Using foil lifting handle, place bowl on rack in cooker, folding handle ends down over bowl (see page 7).

2 Close cover securely. Cook over **high** heat until pressure regulator begins to rock. **Lower heat and cook 12 minutes with pressure regulator rocking slowly.**

3 **Cool cooker at once under cold running water.** Open cooker. Use lifting handle to carefully remove bowl from cooker; remove foil. Stir in ³⁄₄ cup water, brown rice, parsley, onion, butter, brown sugar, thyme, black pepper, and red pepper. Cover bowl firmly with aluminum foil. Add ¹⁄₂ cup water to cooker. Using foil lifting handle, place bowl on rack in cooker, folding handle ends down over bowl.

4 Close cover securely. Place pressure regulator on vent pipe. Continue cooking over **high** heat until pressure regulator begins to rock. **Lower heat and cook 12 minutes with pressure regulator rocking slowly.**

5 **Remove from heat and let stand until cover lock drops.** Open cooker. Use lifting handle to carefully remove bowl from cooker; remove foil. Stir in orange juice, apricots, cranberries, and raisins; allow to steam 5 minutes. Fluff rice gently with fork before serving.

Black Bean Chili

makes 6 to 8 servings

1	pound dried black beans
8	cups water, divided
1	can (14$^1/_2$ ounces) diced tomatoes, undrained
2	large onions, chopped
2	jalapeño peppers,* stemmed, seeded, and minced
3	cloves garlic, minced
2	tablespoons chili powder
1$^1/_2$	teaspoons salt
1	teaspoon ground paprika
1	teaspoon dried oregano
1	teaspoon unsweetened cocoa powder
$^1/_2$	teaspoon ground cumin
$^1/_4$	teaspoon ground cinnamon
1	bay leaf
1	tablespoon red wine vinegar
	Plain yogurt or sour cream, picante sauce, sliced green onions, chopped fresh cilantro (optional)

Jalapeño peppers can sting and irritate the skin, so wear rubber gloves when handling peppers and do not touch your eyes.

1 Rinse beans thoroughly in colander under cold running water, picking out any debris or blemished beans. Combine beans and 6 cups water. Soak 6 to 8 hours or overnight. After soaking, rinse and drain beans, and remove any loose skins.

2 Combine beans, 2 cups water, tomatoes, onions, jalapeños, garlic, chili powder, salt, paprika, oregano, cocoa, cumin, cinnamon, and bay leaf in cooker; stir well.

3 Close cover securely. Place pressure regulator on vent pipe. Cook over **high** heat until pressure regulator begins to rock. **Lower heat and cook 4 minutes with pressure regulator rocking slowly.**

4 **Cool cooker at once under cold running water.** Open cooker. Stir in vinegar before serving chili with desired garnishes.

PRESTO
Tip For a heartier meal, hollow out small loaves of sourdough bread or crusty bread and serve chili in bread "bowl."

Winter Squash Risotto

2	tablespoons olive oil
2	cups butternut or delicata squash (1 small butternut squash or 1 medium delicata), peeled and cut into $1/2$-inch pieces
1	large shallot or small onion, finely chopped
1	cup arborio rice
3	cups vegetable or chicken broth*
1	teaspoon salt
$1/2$	teaspoon ground paprika
$1/4$	teaspoon dried thyme
$1/4$	teaspoon black pepper
$1/4$	cup dry white wine (optional)*
2	cups water
$1/2$	to 1 cup grated Parmesan or Romano cheese
	Shredded Parmesan or Romano cheese (optional)

***If using wine, reduce broth to $2^3/_4$ cups.**

1 Heat oil in cooker over medium heat. Add squash and shallot; cook and stir 5 minutes. Add rice and stir 2 minutes or until coated and slightly translucent. Combine squash, shallot, rice, broth, salt, paprika, thyme, pepper, and wine, if desired, in metal bowl that fits loosely in cooker. Cover bowl firmly with aluminum foil. Pour water into cooker. Using foil lifting handle, place bowl on rack in cooker, folding handle ends down over bowl (see page 7).

2 Close cover securely. Place pressure regulator on vent pipe. Cook over **high** heat until pressure regulator begins to rock. **Lower heat and cook 8 minutes with pressure regulator rocking slowly.**

3 Remove from heat and let stand until cover lock drops. Open cooker. Use lifting handle to carefully remove bowl from cooker; remove foil. Stir in grated Parmesan cheese, to taste. Garnish with additional cheese, if desired.

PRESTO
Tip **If you're using an oven-safe glass bowl instead of a metal bowl, increase the cooking time 4 to 5 minutes because glass takes longer to heat than metal.**

Easy Herbed Rice

makes 4 servings

3½	**cups water, divided**
¾	**cup white rice**
1	**tablespoon minced onion**
1	**tablespoon unsalted butter**
1	**large clove garlic, minced**
¼	**teaspoon salt**
1	**tablespoon minced fresh parsley**
1	**tablespoon minced fresh basil or 1 teaspoon dried basil***
1	**tablespoon minced fresh marjoram or 1 teaspoon dried marjoram***

***If using dried herbs, add to rice before cooking.**

1 Combine 1½ cups water, rice, onion, butter, garlic, and salt in metal bowl that fits loosely in cooker. Cover bowl firmly with aluminum foil. Pour 2 cups water into cooker. Using foil lifting handle, place bowl on rack in cooker, folding handle ends down over bowl (see page 7).

2 Close cover securely. Place pressure regulator on vent pipe. Cook over **high** heat until pressure regulator begins to rock. **Lower heat and cook 5 minutes with pressure regulator rocking slowly.**

3 **Remove from heat and let stand until cover lock drops.** Open cooker. Use lifting handle to carefully remove bowl from cooker; remove foil. Drain any remaining water from rice. Stir in parsley, basil, and marjoram. Fluff rice gently with fork before serving.

PRESTO *Tip*
To make this recipe with brown rice, follow the same procedure, but cook for 10 minutes with the pressure regulator rocking slowly.

Spinach Parmesan Risotto

1	tablespoon olive oil
1	cup arborio rice
3	cups chicken broth
1/2	teaspoon salt
1/2	teaspoon white pepper
2	cups water
1 1/2	cups chopped fresh spinach
1/2	cup fresh or frozen peas, thawed
1/2	cup grated Parmesan cheese
1	teaspoon grated lemon peel

1 Heat oil in cooker over medium heat. Add rice; cook and stir 2 minutes or until coated and slightly translucent. Place rice, broth, salt, and pepper in metal bowl that fits loosely in cooker. Cover bowl firmly with aluminum foil. Pour water into cooker. Using foil lifting handle, place bowl on rack in cooker, folding handle ends down over bowl (see page 7).

2 Close cover securely. Place pressure regulator on vent pipe. Cook over **high** heat until pressure regulator begins to rock. **Lower heat and cook 8 minutes with pressure regulator rocking slowly.**

3 **Remove from heat and let stand until cover lock drops.** Open cooker. Use lifting handle to carefully remove bowl from cooker; remove foil. Stir in spinach and peas. Cover with foil; let stand 5 minutes or until spinach and peas are heated through. Stir in Parmesan and lemon peel.

PRESTO *Tip* For color and variety, you can substitute any frozen vegetable medley that includes diced or shredded vegetables in place of the peas. Just be sure the vegetables are completely thawed and at room temperature before adding them to the risotto.

Risotto with Mushrooms and Sun-Dried Tomatoes

makes 4 to 6 servings

1	tablespoon olive oil
2	teaspoons butter
1	cup arborio rice
¼	cup minced shallot or onion
2⅓	cups chicken broth
½	cup chopped dried mushrooms
¼	cup chopped sun-dried tomatoes (not oil-packed)
2	cups water
½	cup shredded Parmesan cheese
2	tablespoons pine nuts
2	tablespoons chopped fresh chives

1 Heat oil and butter in cooker over medium heat. Add rice; cook and stir 2 minutes or until coated and slightly translucent. Add shallot; cook 1 minute, stirring constantly. Combine rice, shallot, broth, mushrooms, and tomatoes in metal bowl that fits loosely in cooker. Cover bowl firmly with aluminum foil. Pour water into cooker. Using foil lifting handle, place bowl on rack in cooker, folding handle ends down over bowl (see page 7).

2 Close cover securely. Place pressure regulator on vent pipe. Cook over **high** heat until pressure regulator begins to rock. **Lower heat and cook 8 minutes with pressure regulator rocking slowly.**

3 **Remove from heat and let stand until cover lock drops.** Open cooker. Use lifting handle to carefully remove bowl from cooker; remove foil. Stir in Parmesan cheese, pine nuts, and chives.

PRESTO
Tip

Add freshness, color, and full flavor by adding fresh herbs to foods just before you serve them.

Vegetable *Variety*

Lemon Parmesan Cauliflower

makes 6 servings

1	cup water
3	tablespoons chopped fresh parsley
$^1/_2$	teaspoon grated lemon peel
1	large head cauliflower, trimmed
1	tablespoon butter
3	cloves garlic, minced
2	tablespoons fresh lemon juice
$^1/_4$	teaspoon salt
$^1/_4$	cup shredded or grated Parmesan cheese

PRESTO *Tip*  For cauliflower that's a little more al dente, cook a 2$^1/_2$-pound head for 1 to 2 minutes under pressure.

1 Pour water into cooker. Stir in parsley and lemon peel. Using foil lifting handle, place cauliflower on rack in cooker, folding handle ends down over cauliflower (see page 7). Close cover securely. Place pressure regulator on vent pipe. Cook over **high** heat until pressure regulator begins to rock. **Lower heat and cook 3 minutes with pressure regulator rocking slowly.**

2 **Cool cooker at once under cold running water.** Open cooker. Use lifting handle to carefully remove rack with cauliflower from cooker. Place cauliflower in large bowl. Reserve $^1/_2$ cup cooking liquid; discard remaining liquid.

3 Heat butter in cooker over medium heat. Add garlic; cook and stir 1 minute or until fragrant. Stir in lemon juice, salt, and reserved $^1/_2$ cup cooking liquid. Spoon lemon sauce over cauliflower. Sprinkle with Parmesan cheese before serving.

Brussels Sprouts in Orange Sauce

makes 4 servings

4	cups fresh Brussels sprouts
1/2	cup plus 2 tablespoons unsweetened orange juice, divided
1/4	teaspoon crushed red pepper flakes
1/4	teaspoon ground cinnamon
	Salt and black pepper, to taste
1	to 2 teaspoons cornstarch
1	teaspoon honey
1	teaspoon shredded or grated orange peel

1 Trim stems from Brussels sprouts and pull off any outer discolored leaves.

2 Combine $\frac{1}{2}$ cup orange juice, red pepper flakes, cinnamon, and salt and pepper in cooker. Stir in Brussels sprouts.

3 Close cover securely. Place pressure regulator on vent pipe. Cook over **high** heat until pressure regulator begins to rock. **Lower heat and cook 1 to 2 minutes with pressure regulator rocking slowly.**

4 **Cool cooker at once under cold running water.** Open cooker. Transfer Brussels sprouts to serving bowl with slotted spoon. Combine remaining 2 tablespoons orange juice and cornstarch in small bowl; mix until smooth. Add honey, orange peel, and cornstarch mixture to cooker. Cook and stir over medium-high heat until thickened. Pour sauce over Brussels sprouts; toss lightly to coat evenly.

PRESTO Tip

When shredding or grating an orange, avoid the bitter white pith under the peel. The best flavor comes from the oils that are found only in the colored part of the peel.

Coconut Butternut Squash

makes 5 to 6 servings

1	tablespoon butter
$\frac{1}{2}$	cup chopped onion
1	butternut squash (about 3 pounds), peeled, seeded, and cut into 1-inch pieces
1	can (13$\frac{1}{2}$ ounces) coconut milk*
3	tablespoons packed light brown sugar, divided
1	teaspoon salt
$\frac{1}{2}$	teaspoon ground cinnamon
$\frac{1}{4}$	teaspoon ground nutmeg
$\frac{1}{4}$	teaspoon ground allspice
2	teaspoons grated fresh ginger

Shake vigorously before opening to mix thoroughly.

1 Melt butter in cooker over medium heat. Add onion; cook and stir 4 minutes or until soft. Stir in squash, coconut milk, 1 tablespoon brown sugar, salt, cinnamon, nutmeg, and allspice.

2 Close cover securely. Place pressure regulator on vent pipe. Continue cooking over **high** heat until pressure regulator begins to rock. **Lower heat and cook 6 minutes with pressure regulator rocking slowly.**

3 **Cool cooker at once under cold running water.** Open cooker and stir in ginger. Pour into blender or food processor and process until smooth. Spoon into shallow serving bowl or individual custard bowls. Sprinkle evenly with remaining 2 tablespoons brown sugar.

Balsamic Green Beans with Almonds

1	**cup water**
1	**pound fresh green beans, trimmed**
2	**teaspoons olive oil**
2	**teaspoons balsamic vinegar**
1/2	**teaspoon salt**
1/4	**teaspoon black pepper**
2	**tablespoons sliced almonds, toasted***

**Toast almonds in a dry skillet over medium heat 3 to 5 minutes or until fragrant, stirring frequently. Cool before using.*

1 Pour water into cooker. Place beans on rack in cooker. Close cover securely. Place pressure regulator on vent pipe. Cook over **high** heat until pressure regulator begins to rock. **Lower heat and cook 2 minutes with pressure regulator rocking slowly.**

2 **Cool cooker at once under cold running water.** Open cooker. Drain beans, remove rack, and return beans to cooker. Add oil, vinegar, salt, and pepper and toss to coat evenly. Before serving, sprinkle with almonds.

Cider Vinaigrette-Glazed Beets

makes 8 servings

6	medium red and/or golden beets
1½	cups water
1	tablespoon olive oil
1	tablespoon cider vinegar
½	teaspoon prepared horseradish
½	teaspoon Dijon mustard
¼	teaspoon firmly packed brown sugar
	Salt and black pepper, to taste
⅓	cup crumbled blue cheese (optional)

1 Cut tops off beets, leaving at least 1 inch of stems. Scrub beets under running water with soft vegetable brush, being careful not to break skins. Pour water into cooker. Place beets on rack in cooker.

2 Close cover securely. Place pressure regulator on vent pipe. Cook over **high** heat until pressure regulator begins to rock. **Lower heat and cook 15 minutes with pressure regulator rocking slowly.**

3 **Cool cooker at once under cold running water.** Open cooker. Remove beets; allow to cool slightly.

4 Blend oil, vinegar, horseradish, mustard, brown sugar, and salt and pepper in medium bowl.

5 When beets are cool enough to handle, peel off skins and trim root ends. Cut into wedges and place warm beets in vinaigrette mixture; toss gently to coat. Sprinkle evenly with cheese, if desired. Serve warm or at room temperature.

PRESTO *Tip*

The cooking time depends on the size of the beets, which can vary slightly. If beets are not tender enough, close cover and cook under pressure 1 or 2 minutes longer.

Low-Carb Mashed "Potatoes"

makes 6 servings

2	**heads cauliflower (about 8 cups florets)**
1	**cup water**
2	**tablespoons butter**
1	**tablespoon half-and-half**
	Salt and black pepper, to taste

If you prefer to use an immersion blender, drain the cooking liquid first, then proceed as directed.

1 Remove cores from cauliflower heads and break into equal-size florets. Pour water into cooker. Place florets on rack in cooker.

2 Close cover securely. Place pressure regulator on vent pipe. Cook over **high** heat until pressure regulator begins to rock. **Lower heat and cook 2 minutes with pressure regulator rocking slowly.**

3 **Cool cooker at once under cold running water.** Open cooker. Place cooked cauliflower in food processor or blender. Process until almost smooth. Add butter. Process until smooth, adding half-and-half as needed to reach desired consistency. Season with salt and pepper.

Lemony Steamed Broccoli

makes 4 servings

1	**pound broccoli**
1	**cup water**
1	**tablespoon butter**
2	**teaspoons lemon juice**
	Salt and black pepper, to taste

1 Break broccoli into florets; discard large stems. Trim smaller stems; cut into thin slices. Place broccoli in steamer basket that fits in cooker. Pour water into cooker. Place basket in cooker.

2 Close cover securely. Place pressure regulator on vent pipe. **Cook over high heat only until pressure regulator begins to rock (0 minutes).**

3 **Cool cooker at once under cold running water.** Open cooker and remove steamer basket. Transfer broccoli to serving bowl. Melt butter and lemon juice in small saucepan over medium heat; pour over broccoli. Season with salt and pepper; toss gently to coat before serving.

Rosemary Garlic Mashed Potatoes

$2^1/_2$ pounds Yukon Gold potatoes (5 medium), peeled and
    diced into 1-inch pieces

$1^1/_2$ cups water

6   to 8 large cloves garlic

$1^1/_2$ teaspoons salt, divided

$^1/_2$ cup milk

$^1/_2$ cup half-and-half

2   tablespoons butter

1   tablespoon minced fresh rosemary leaves or
    1 teaspoon dried rosemary

$^1/_8$ teaspoon white pepper

1 Place potatoes, water, garlic, and 1 teaspoon salt in cooker. Close cover securely. Place pressure regulator on vent pipe. Cook over **high** heat until pressure regulator begins to rock. **Lower heat and cook 5 minutes with pressure regulator rocking slowly.**

2 **Cool cooker at once under cold running water.** Open cooker. Drain potatoes and garlic, and return to cooker. Combine milk, half-and-half, butter, rosemary, remaining $^1/_2$ teaspoon salt, and pepper in small saucepan over medium-high heat. Cook and stir 3 minutes or until butter has melted and mixture has come to a simmer. Mash potatoes and garlic with potato masher until smooth. Stir in milk mixture with rubber spatula until smooth. Serve immediately.

Sweet and Sour Red Cabbage

makes 8 servings

2	thick slices bacon, chopped
1	cup chopped onion
8	cups thinly sliced red cabbage
2	unpeeled large tart apples, cored and cut into chunks
$\frac{1}{2}$	cup honey
$\frac{1}{2}$	cup cider vinegar
$\frac{1}{4}$	cup water
1	teaspoon salt
1	teaspoon celery salt
$\frac{1}{4}$	teaspoon black pepper
3	tablespoons cold water
2	tablespoons all-purpose flour

1 Fry bacon in cooker over medium heat until crisp. Remove bacon with slotted spoon to paper towels. Cook and stir onion in bacon drippings 2 minutes or until soft. Add cabbage, apples, honey, vinegar, water, salt, celery salt, and pepper.

2 Close cover securely. Place pressure regulator on vent pipe. Continue cooking over **high** heat until pressure regulator begins to rock. **Lower heat and cook 4 minutes with pressure regulator rocking slowly.**

3 **Cool cooker at once under cold running water.** Open cooker. Combine flour and water. Mix smooth and add to cooker. Cook and stir, uncovered, over medium-high heat until sauce has thickened. Sprinkle with bacon before serving warm.

Broth-Braised Brussels Sprouts

makes 4 servings

4	cups fresh Brussels sprouts
1	cup condensed beef broth
1	tablespoon butter, softened
	Salt and black pepper, to taste
¼	cup grated Parmesan cheese
	Ground paprika (optional)

1 Trim stems from Brussels sprouts and pull off any outer discolored leaves. Pour broth into cooker. Place Brussels sprouts on rack in cooker.

2 Close cover securely. Place pressure regulator on vent pipe. Cook over **high** heat until pressure regulator begins to rock. **Lower heat and cook 2 minutes with pressure regulator rocking slowly.**

3 **Cool cooker at once under cold running water.** Open cooker. Transfer Brussels sprouts to serving bowl with slotted spoon. Add 2 tablespoons broth from cooker; discard any remaining broth. Add butter, salt, and pepper; toss lightly to coat evenly. Sprinkle with Parmesan cheese and paprika, if desired.

PRESTO
Tip **For more even cooking, cut an X deep into the stem end of each Brussels sprout.**

Spicy Oriental Green Beans

1   cup water

1   pound whole green beans, trimmed

2   tablespoons chopped green onions

2   tablespoons dry sherry or chicken broth

4½   teaspoons reduced-sodium soy sauce

1   teaspoon chili sauce with garlic

1   teaspoon dark sesame oil

1   clove garlic, minced

1 Pour water into cooker. Place beans on rack in cooker. Close cover securely. Place pressure regulator on vent pipe. Cook over **high** heat until pressure regulator begins to rock. **Lower heat and cook 2 minutes with pressure regulator rocking slowly.**

2 **Cool cooker at once under cold running water.** Open cooker. Drain beans; set aside in large bowl. Remove rack from cooker. Combine green onions, sherry, soy sauce, chili sauce, sesame oil, and garlic in cooker. Cook and stir 1 minute or until heated through. Pour sauce over beans and toss to coat evenly.

Smashed Potatoes

3/4   pound small red potatoes (6 to 8), unpeeled, washed, and cut in half

1   cup water

3   tablespoons sour cream, buttermilk, or whipping cream

3   tablespoons unsalted butter

1   tablespoon milk

       Salt, to taste

1   tablespoon chopped fresh chives (optional)

1 Place potatoes and water in cooker. Close cover securely. Place pressure regulator on vent pipe. Cook over **high** heat until pressure regulator begins to rock. **Lower heat and cook 5 minutes with pressure regulator rocking slowly.**

2 **Cool cooker at once under cold running water.** Open cooker. Drain potatoes and return to cooker. Add sour cream, butter, and milk. Mash with potato masher until blended. Season with salt. Sprinkle with chives, if desired.

Sherried Carrots

makes 4 servings

1   pound baby carrots

1/2   cup dry sherry

1/4   cup water

2   teaspoons butter

       Salt and black pepper, to taste

1   tablespoon minced fresh parsley

1 Place carrots, sherry, water, butter, and salt and pepper in cooker. Close cover securely. Place pressure regulator on vent pipe. Cook over **high** heat until pressure regulator begins to rock. **Lower heat and cook 4 minutes with pressure regulator rocking slowly.**

2 **Cool cooker at once under cold running water.** Open cooker. Season with salt and pepper. Simmer, uncovered, 5 minutes or until liquid has reduced to a glaze. Sprinkle with parsley before serving.

Dessert Express

Mocha Custard

makes 6 servings

2	cups half-and-half
4	eggs
½	cup granulated sugar
1	tablespoon instant espresso coffee granules
1	tablespoon unsweetened cocoa powder
1	cup water
	Chocolate curls or chocolate-covered coffee beans (optional)
	Shredded or grated orange peel (optional)

1 Combine half-and-half, eggs, sugar, espresso, and cocoa in blender jar. Blend ingredients well, using several short bursts.

2 Pour into six individual custard cups, filling two-thirds full. Cover each cup firmly with aluminum foil. Pour water into cooker. Place three custard cups on rack in cooker. Stack remaining three custard cups, staggering around bottom three custard cups so edges support upper custard cups.

3 Close cover securely. Place pressure regulator on vent pipe. Cook over **high** heat until pressure regulator begins to rock. **Lower heat and cook 5 minutes with pressure regulator rocking slowly.**

4 **Cool cooker at once under cold running water.** Open cooker and carefully remove custard cups. Serve warm or at room temperature. Garnish with chocolate curls and orange peel, if desired.

Cinnamon Raisin Bread Pudding with Vanilla Rum Sauce

4	to 5 cups day-old French bread, cut into 1-inch cubes
1	cup raisins
1	cup milk
1	cup low-fat evaporated milk
2	large eggs
1	egg yolk
1/4	cup granulated sugar
1/8	teaspoon ground cinnamon
1/8	teaspoon ground nutmeg
1/2	tablespoon butter
2 1/2	cups water
	Vanilla Rum Sauce (recipe follows)

1 Place bread cubes in lightly greased baking dish or metal bowl that fits loosely in cooker. Add raisins; toss to blend in evenly.

2 Combine milk, evaporated milk, eggs, egg yolk, sugar, cinnamon, and nutmeg in medium bowl; whisk until frothy. Pour over bread. Using whisk, push bread down to soak evenly.

3 Rub butter in circle large enough to cover top of baking dish onto large piece of aluminum foil. Cover dish firmly with foil, butter side down. Pour water into cooker. Using foil lifting handle, place dish on rack in cooker, folding handle ends down over dish (see page 7).

4 Close cover securely. Place pressure regulator on vent pipe. Cook over **high** heat until pressure regulator begins to rock. **Lower heat and cook 15 minutes with pressure regulator rocking slowly.**

5 **Remove from heat and let stand until cover lock drops.** Open cooker. Use lifting handle to carefully remove dish; remove foil. Stir and serve warm with Vanilla Rum Sauce.

Vanilla Rum Sauce

2	egg yolks
$^1/_4$	cup granulated sugar
1	cup heavy whipping cream
$^1/_4$	teaspoon vanilla extract
2	tablespoons dark rum, brandy, or Grand Marnier

1 Whip egg yolks and sugar together until light and fluffy; set aside.

2 Scald cream and vanilla in medium saucepan. When cream begins to boil along sides of pan, whisk yolk mixture into cream. Cook over high heat 2 minutes, whipping constantly with whisk. Remove from heat and strain through fine strainer to remove any lumps, if necessary. Mix in rum. Serve warm or at room temperature over bread pudding.

makes 1$^1/_4$ cups

Custard Brûlée

5	eggs
1/2	cup granulated sugar
3	cups milk
1	teaspoon vanilla extract
1/2	teaspoon ground cinnamon
	Ground nutmeg (optional)
1	cup water
1/4	cup packed light brown sugar

1 Beat eggs and sugar in medium bowl with electric mixer at medium speed 5 minutes or until slightly thickened. Gradually beat in milk and vanilla. Pour into 1½-quart soufflé dish or round casserole that fits loosely in cooker. Sprinkle lightly with cinnamon and nutmeg, if desired.

2 Cover dish firmly with aluminum foil. Pour water into cooker. Using foil lifting handle, place dish on rack in cooker, folding handle ends down over dish (see page 7).

3 Close cover securely. Place pressure regulator on vent pipe. Cook over **high** heat until pressure regulator begins to rock. **Lower heat and cook 15 minutes with pressure regulator rocking slowly.**

4 **Cool cooker at once under cold running water.** Open cooker. Use lifting handle to carefully remove dish; remove foil. Cool to room temperature on wire rack. Cover; refrigerate 3 to 4 hours or until well chilled.

5 Before serving, preheat broiler. Sprinkle brown sugar evenly over top (press sugar through sieve to remove any lumps, if necessary). Broil 4 inches from heat 2 to 3 minutes or until sugar is melted and caramelized. Serve immediately.

PRESTO *Tip*
If you have a culinary torch, use it to melt the brown sugar on the custard instead of broiling.

Very Berry Cheesecake

makes 6 to 8 servings

Crust

¾	cup cinnamon or chocolate graham cracker crumbs (about 5 whole crackers)
2	tablespoons butter, melted

Cheesecake

1	package (8 ounces) cream cheese, at room temperature
1	package (3 ounces) cream cheese, at room temperature
½	cup granulated sugar
2	eggs, at room temperature
1	teaspoon vanilla extract
1	cup fresh blueberries*
2	cups water

Topping

⅓	cup currant jelly or seedless raspberry jam
1	to 1¼ cups fresh raspberries*

If blueberries or raspberries are unavailable, substitute seasonal berries or a mix of berries.

1 Cut parchment paper to fit inside 7½-inch springform or cheesecake pan that fits loosely in cooker. Lightly coat bottom and sides of pan with nonstick cooking spray. Combine cracker crumbs and melted butter in small bowl. Pat mixture onto bottom and about ¼ inch up side of prepared pan. Refrigerate until needed.

2 Beat cream cheese and sugar in large bowl with electric mixer at medium-high speed until light and fluffy. Add eggs, one at a time, blending well after each addition. Stir in vanilla. Sprinkle blueberries evenly into prepared pan. Pour batter into pan, pushing blueberries into batter, if necessary.

3 Cover pan bottom and top firmly with aluminum foil. (Use large foil sheet on bottom to prevent water from leaking into springform pan.) Pour water into cooker. Using foil lifting handle, place pan on rack in cooker, folding handle ends down over pan (see page 7).

4 Close cover securely. Place pressure regulator on vent pipe. Cook over **high** heat until pressure regulator begins to rock. **Lower heat and cook 30 minutes with pressure regulator rocking slowly.**

5 **Cool cooker at once under cold running water.** Open cooker. Use lifting handle to carefully remove pan; remove foil. Cool cheesecake at room temperature 1 hour; refrigerate 2 to 3 hours. Run thin knife around edge of cheesecake to loosen; remove side and bottom of pan, peeling parchment paper off bottom. Heat jelly in small saucepan or in glass measuring cup in microwave, stirring until smooth. Spoon over cheesecake. Arrange raspberries on top of cheesecake. Refrigerate leftovers.

Baked Applesauce Custard

makes 6 servings

1½	**cups unsweetened applesauce**
½	**teaspoon ground cinnamon**
¼	**teaspoon salt**
4	**eggs**
½	**cup half-and-half**
¼	**cup unsweetened apple juice concentrate**
¼	**teaspoon ground nutmeg**
1	**cup water**

1 Combine applesauce, cinnamon, and salt in medium bowl. Whisk in eggs, half-and-half, and apple juice concentrate; mix well. Pour into 1½-quart soufflé dish or round casserole that fits loosely in cooker. Sprinkle evenly with nutmeg.

2 Cover bowl firmly with aluminum foil. Pour water into cooker. Using foil lifting handle, place dish on rack in cooker, folding handle ends down over dish (see page 7).

3 Close cover securely. Place pressure regulator on vent pipe. Cook over **high** heat until pressure regulator begins to rock. **Lower heat and cook 15 minutes with pressure regulator rocking slowly.**

4 **Cool cooker at once under cold running water.** Open cooker. Use lifting handle to carefully remove dish; remove foil. Cool on wire rack.

Petite Pumpkin Custards

makes 8 servings

1 **can (16 ounces) solid-pack pumpkin**

1 **can (14 ounces) sweetened condensed milk (NOT evaporated milk)**

3 **eggs, beaten**

1 **teaspoon ground cinnamon**

1 **teaspoon finely chopped candied ginger (optional)**

1/4 **teaspoon ground cloves**

1 **cup water**

 Whipped cream (optional)

1 Combine pumpkin, condensed milk, eggs, cinnamon, ginger, if desired, and cloves; mix until smooth. Pour into eight individual custard cups. Cover each cup firmly with aluminum foil. Pour water into cooker. Place four custard cups on rack in cooker. Stack remaining four custard cups, staggering around bottom four custard cups so edges support upper custard cups. (Custard may be cooked in two batches, if desired.)

2 Close cover securely. Place pressure regulator on vent pipe. Cook over **high** heat until pressure regulator begins to rock. **Lower heat and cook 10 minutes with pressure regulator rocking slowly.**

3 **Cool cooker at once under cold running water.** Open cooker. Carefully remove custard cups; remove foil. Refrigerate until chilled. Serve with whipped cream, if desired.

Chocolate Rice Pudding

makes 6 servings

2¹/₂	cups water, divided

2½   cups water, divided

1   cup long-grain white rice

1½   cups milk

½   cup plus 1 tablespoon granulated sugar, divided

2   tablespoons cornstarch

¼   teaspoon salt

½   cup semisweet chocolate chips

½   cup whipping cream

1   bar (3 ounces) premium semisweet chocolate, shaved into chocolate curls (optional)

1 Combine 1½ cups water and rice in metal bowl that fits loosely in cooker. Cover bowl firmly with aluminum foil. Pour 1 cup water into cooker. Using foil lifting handle, place bowl on rack in cooker, folding handle ends down (see page 7).

2 Close cover securely. Place pressure regulator on vent pipe. Cook over **high** heat until pressure regulator begins to rock. **Lower heat and cook 10 minutes with pressure regulator rocking slowly.**

3 **Cool cooker at once under cold running water.** Open cooker. Use lifting handle to carefully remove bowl from cooker; remove foil. Blend milk, ½ cup sugar, cornstarch, and salt in small bowl. Stir into cooked rice. Stir in chocolate chips. Cover bowl firmly with aluminum foil. Using foil lifting handle, place bowl on rack in cooker, folding handle ends down over bowl.

4 Close cover securely. Place pressure regulator on vent pipe. Cook over **high** heat until pressure regulator begins to rock. **Lower heat and cook 5 minutes with pressure regulator rocking slowly.**

5 **Cool cooker at once under cold running water.** Open cooker. Use lifting handle to carefully remove bowl from cooker; remove foil. Spoon pudding into six custard cups. Let stand 10 minutes.

6 Beat whipping cream in chilled small bowl with electric mixer at medium speed until soft peaks form. Add remaining 1 tablespoon sugar; beat until stiff. Top pudding with whipped cream and chocolate curls, if desired.

PRESTO

Tip

For chocolate decorations, start with a chocolate bar at room temperature. Run a vegetable peeler along the top of the chocolate bar to make curls, or the edge to make shavings.

Index

METRIC CONVERSION CHART

VOLUME MEASUREMENTS (dry)

$\frac{1}{8}$ teaspoon = 0.5 mL
$\frac{1}{4}$ teaspoon = 1 mL
$\frac{1}{2}$ teaspoon = 2 mL
$\frac{3}{4}$ teaspoon = 4 mL
1 teaspoon = 5 mL
1 tablespoon = 15 mL
2 tablespoons = 30 mL
$\frac{1}{4}$ cup = 60 mL
$\frac{1}{3}$ cup = 75 mL
$\frac{1}{2}$ cup = 125 mL
$\frac{2}{3}$ cup = 150 mL
$\frac{3}{4}$ cup = 175 mL
1 cup = 250 mL
2 cups = 1 pint = 500 mL
3 cups = 750 mL
4 cups = 1 quart = 1 L

VOLUME MEASUREMENTS (fluid)

1 fluid ounce (2 tablespoons) = 30 mL
4 fluid ounces ($\frac{1}{2}$ cup) = 125 mL
8 fluid ounces (1 cup) = 250 mL
12 fluid ounces (1$\frac{1}{2}$ cups) = 375 mL
16 fluid ounces (2 cups) = 500 mL

WEIGHTS (mass)

$\frac{1}{2}$ ounce = 15 g
1 ounce = 30 g
3 ounces = 90 g
4 ounces = 120 g
8 ounces = 225 g
10 ounces = 285 g
12 ounces = 360 g
16 ounces = 1 pound = 450 g

DIMENSIONS

$\frac{1}{16}$ inch = 2 mm
$\frac{1}{8}$ inch = 3 mm
$\frac{1}{4}$ inch = 6 mm
$\frac{1}{2}$ inch = 1.5 cm
$\frac{3}{4}$ inch = 2 cm
1 inch = 2.5 cm

OVEN TEMPERATURES

250°F = 120°C
275°F = 140°C
300°F = 150°C
325°F = 160°C
350°F = 180°C
375°F = 190°C
400°F = 200°C
425°F = 220°C
450°F = 230°C

BAKING PAN SIZES

Utensil	Size in Inches/Quarts	Metric Volume	Size in Centimeters
Baking or	8 × 8 × 2	2 L	20 × 20 × 5
Cake Pan	9 × 9 × 2	2.5 L	23 × 23 × 5
(square or	12 × 8 × 2	3 L	30 × 20 × 5
rectangular)	13 × 9 × 2	3.5 L	33 × 23 × 5
Loaf Pan	8 × 4 × 3	1.5 L	20 × 10 × 7
	9 × 5 × 3	2 L	23 × 13 × 7
Round Layer	8 × 1½	1.2 L	20 × 4
Cake Pan	9 × 1½	1.5 L	23 × 4
Pie Plate	8 × 1¼	750 mL	20 × 3
	9 × 1¼	1 L	23 × 3
Baking Dish	1 quart	1 L	—
or Casserole	1½ quarts	1.5 L	—
	2 quarts	2 L	—